# Best Editorial Cartoons of the Year

JOE MAJESKI
Courtesy Times-Leader (Pa.)

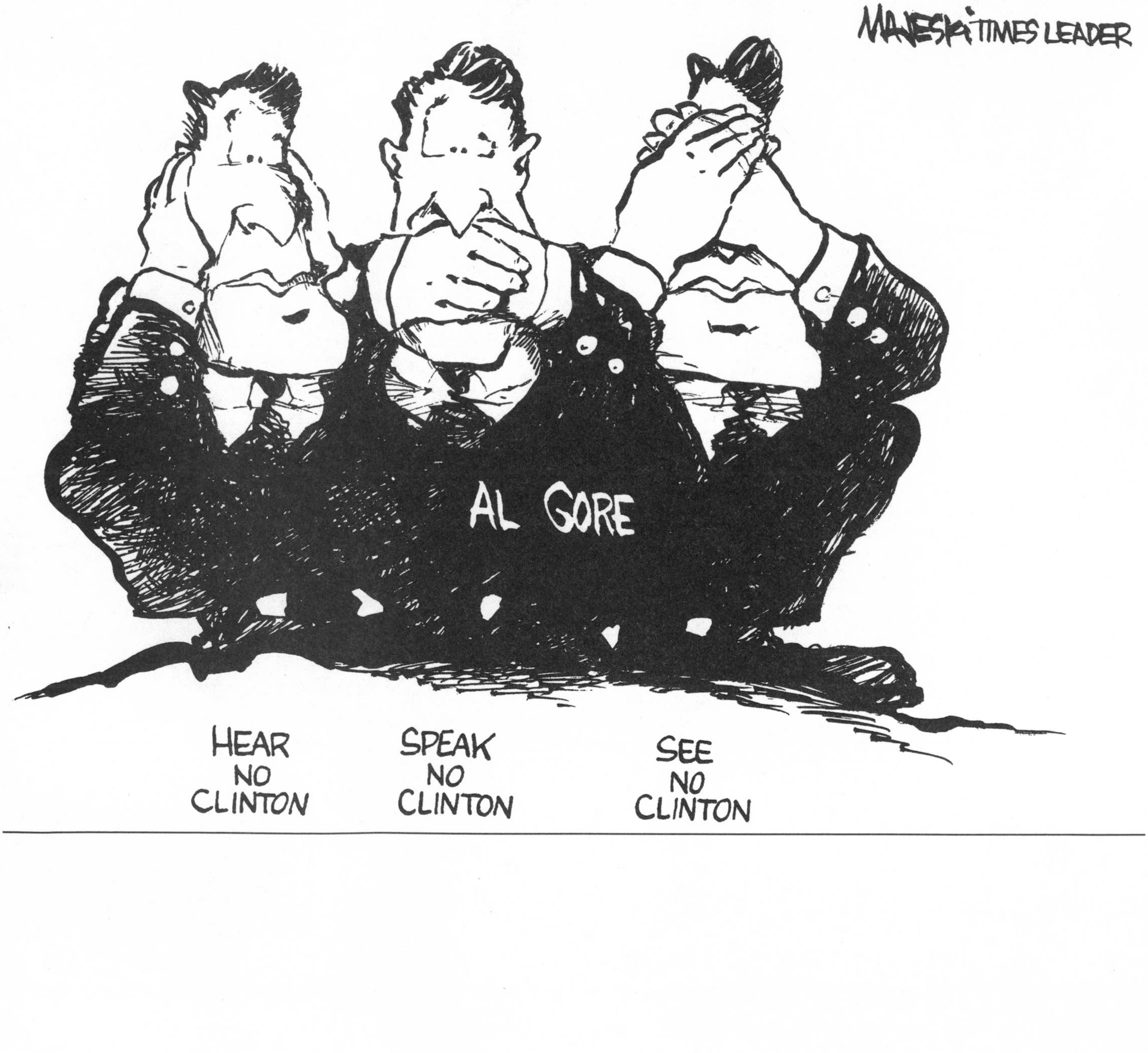
MAJESKI TIMES LEADER
AL GORE
HEAR NO CLINTON
SPEAK NO CLINTON
SEE NO CLINTON

# BEST EDITORIAL CARTOONS OF THE YEAR

## 2001 EDITION

Edited by
**CHARLES BROOKS**

**PELICAN PUBLISHING COMPANY**
Gretna 2001

**Library of Congress Serial Catalog Data**

Best Editorial Cartoons, 1972-
    Gretna [La.} Pelican Pub. Co.
    v. 29 cm. annual-
"A pictorial history of the year."

    1. United States—Politics and government—
1969—Caricatures and Cartoons—Periodicals.
E839.5.B45  320.9'7309240207  73-643645
ISSN 0091-2220                    MARC-S

Manufactured in the United States of America
Published by Pelican Publishing Company, Inc.
1000 Burmaster Street, Gretna, Louisiana 70053

# Contents

JEFF MACNELLY
Courtesy Chicago Tribune

# A Tribute

My very close friend Jeff MacNelly is gone. However, as in John T. McCutcheon's cartoon masterpiece of the passing of the Native American people, the mist still lingers. His cartoons will be missed, but not the memory of that easy-going, infectious, seemingly effortless, albeit dagger-like, go-for-the-jocular style that he brought to the cartoon industry. I—as I suspect many other cartoonists do—have stood by and watched with admiration the impact of Jeff MacNelly's world, not only on us but on the news industry as well.

We are all different, of course, and there are great new powerhouses on line doing super stuff, and that is the way it should be. For a while, the talk was that a lot of us were MacNelly clones, indeed the sincerest form of flattery. This is not the case now. The new styles and political messages penned today are fantastic, but don't you still detect the Jeff MacNelly aroma of booster fuel around the launching pad for these new skyrockets?

I had the privilege of working with Jeff for a number of years at the *Chicago Tribune*. Sharing a tuna salad sandwich over a wastepaper basket on the way to the ever-present deadline gives you a terribly incisive look at a friend's mind; and the view was incredible. We dissected everything: kings, cabbages, B17s, the Cubs, and the business of being totally immersed in the cartoon world.

I guess my real kick was the laughter that came automatically from just being with him. EVERYTHING was funny, from a West Virginian's favorite aromas ("WD-40 and a wet dog") to ". . . any company that can invest in the Chicago Cubs has a view of the future we cannot even begin to comprehend." "Keep honkin' while I reload" was a beautifully lettered bumper sticker on a deliciously rendered rusty old pickup truck. Try not to be influenced by the guy, and try not to miss him.

Jeff's cartoons are unarguably legend and will remain benchmarks for years to come. But first in my mind was that he was a gentle, kind, lovable giant of a man. Ask for anything, and he would give it to you. Just ask any young cartoonist. His insights were more than legend to me because I grew up in the profession admiring his creative processes as well as his abilities to put the results of that intertwining process on paper. Have you ever viewed Jeff MacNelly's fine art paintings? They are lyrical, enticing, and ready to hang on any wall or in any museum. They possess the energy of a Bellows, the force of a Wyeth, and the whimsy of a Rockwell.

Was this sojourn into the colorful arts a release for Jeff from the political black and white—or black and blue—smashmouth, everyday give and take of the editorial cartoon? The answer is YES. What a true delight to watch Jeff's work morph from the goofy gracefulness of the editorial cartoon into a Caribbean pirate in full regalia on a magnificent galleon, sword held high.

As cartoonists, we all take great pride in delivering a political punch. And we know our cartoons can be magical testimonies to our profession. But, above all, we know how lucky we are to be in this crazy art. So let's take a minute and say thanks to Jeff for the great perspective he gave us on this industry. His talent has inspired us to tweak, titillate, and tantalize our public. He gave us immeasurable insights to guide us in a craft that will keep our public coming back for more. To me, that is the ultimate reason we are cartoonists, and as for me personally, what better epitaph for a friend than the image of that gentle giant, pen held skyward, showing us our compass heading.

We miss you, Jeff.

DICK LOCHER
Chicago Tribune

# Award-Winning Cartoons

## 2000 PULITZER PRIZE

## JOEL PETT

Editorial Cartoonist
*Lexington* (Ky.) *Herald-Leader*

Born in Nigeria; editorial cartoonist, *Lexington Herald-Leader*, 1984 to
the present; winner of the 1999 Robert F. Kennedy Award for outstanding
journalistic coverage of the disadvantaged and the 1995 Global Media
Award for cartoons of population issues; past president of the Association
of American Editorial Cartoonists.

# 1999 NATIONAL SOCIETY OF PROFESSIONAL JOURNALISTS AWARD

(Selected in 2000)

## MIKE THOMPSON

Editorial Cartoonist
*Detroit Free Press*

Born in Mankato, Minnesota, 1964; graduate of the University of Wisconsin—Milwaukee in political science; editorial cartoonist, *St. Louis Sun,* 1989-1990, Copley Illinois Newspapers, 1990-1998, and the *Detroit Free Press,* 1998 to the present; cartoons syndicated by Copley News Service; was named 1989 college cartoonist of the year by the Society of Professional Journalists; past winner of the Locher Award, the Charles M. Schulz Award, and the H. L. Mencken Award for editorial cartooning.

# 2000 NATIONAL HEADLINER AWARD

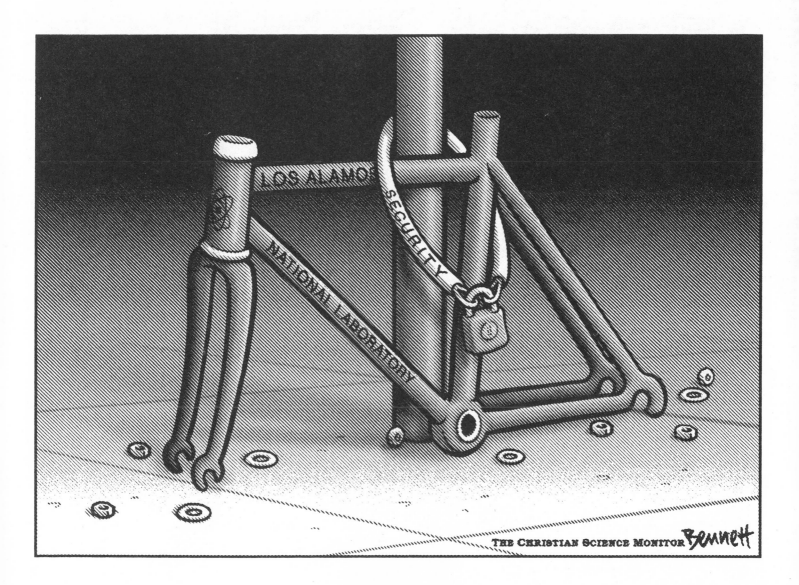

## CLAY BENNETT

Editorial Cartoonist
*Christian Science Monitor*

Graduate of the University of North Alabama, 1980; editorial cartoonist, *St. Petersburg Times,* 1981-1994, and the *Christian Science Monitor,*
1997 to the present; cartoons syndicated by United Media; winner of
the H. L. Mencken Award for editorial cartooning, 1986.

### JIM MORIN

Editorial Cartoonist
*Miami Herald*

Born 1953 in Washington, D. C.; graduate of Syracuse University; editorial cartoonist, *Miami Herald,* 1978 to the present; winner of the Overseas Press Club Award for editorial cartooning, 1979 and 1990, the National Cartoonist Society Award, 1992, the Pulitzer Prize, 1996, the Berryman Award, 1996, and the Thomas Nast Award, 1999; author of three books.

# Best Editorial Cartoons of the Year

DAVE GRANLUND © 2000 METROWEST DAILY NEWS.

DAVE GRANLUND
Courtesy Metrowest Daily News (Mass.)

# The Florida Vote

The blockbuster story of the year 2000 was the razor-thin margin in the U.S. presidential election. Although Democrat Al Gore won the popular vote over Republican George W. Bush by some 500,000 votes, it soon became apparent that neither could win the presidency without Florida's 25 electoral votes. And it was not at all apparent who had won the state.

The Democrats argued that the count was incomplete, especially in Miami-Dade County and Palm Beach County. Florida Secretary of State Katherine Harris, however, certified vote totals that gave Bush a 537-vote victory. A flurry of legal challenges followed, with Gore insisting that voting machines had not properly counted thousands of ballots. The Florida Supreme Court agreed, calling for a manual recount—including an examination of dimples, hanging chads, and semi-perforated ballots—in four disputed counties.

On December 12, 35 days after the election, the U.S. Supreme Court terminated the recount on constitutional grounds, effectively making Bush the winner. The 5-4 decision of the Supreme Court was roundly criticized by Democrat partisans. But Gore delivered a concession speech urging all Americans to support the new president.

WALT HANDELSMAN
Courtesy New Orleans Times-Picayune

15

ED GAMBLE
Courtesy Florida Times-Union

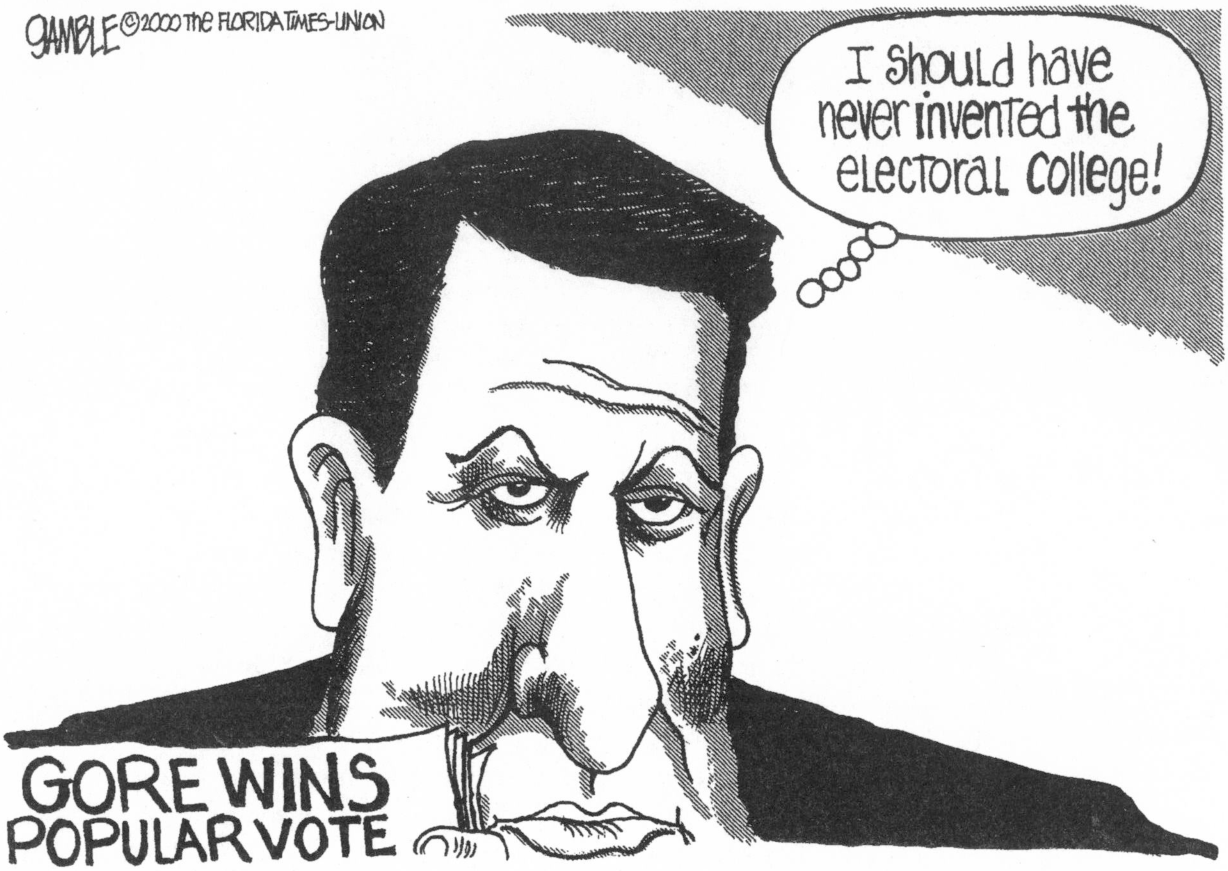
GAMBLE ©2000 THE FLORIDA TIMES-UNION
I should have never invented the electoral college!
GORE WINS POPULAR VOTE

NICK ANDERSON
Courtesy Louisville Courier-Journal

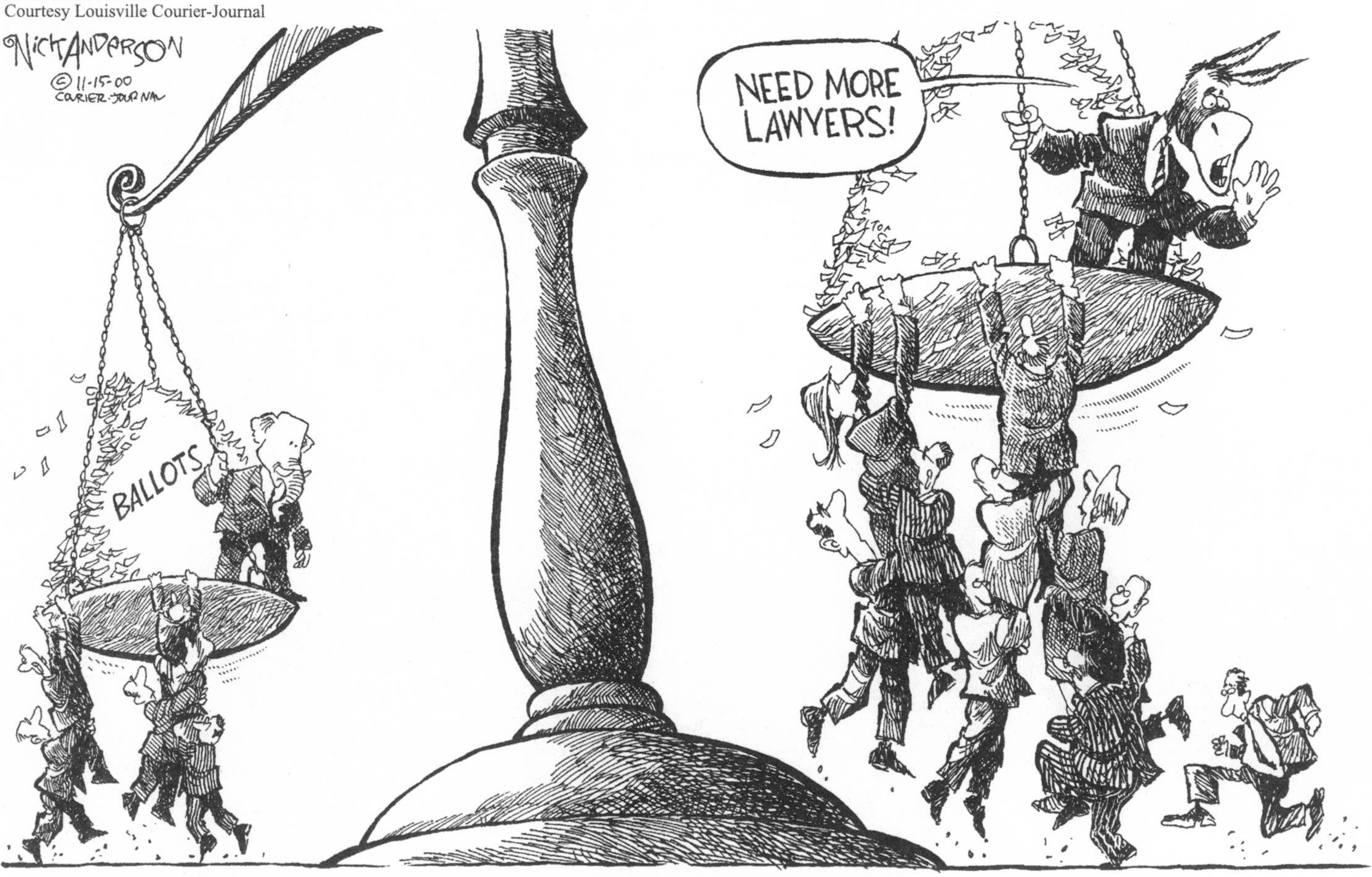
NICK ANDERSON ©11-15-00 COURIER-JOURNAL
NEED MORE LAWYERS!
BALLOTS

ROBERT ARIAIL
Courtesy The State (S.C.)

SVEN VAN ASSCHE
Courtesy Darien Times (Conn.)

17

IF YOU'D TRIED THIS SIX MONTHS AGO...

FELIX PUBLISHING Co.

April 15, 2000

Mr. Felix Arbuthnot
Cleveland, Ohio

Dear Mr. Arbuthnot:

Enclosed, we are returning the manuscript of your novel, "Dead Even." We could, of course, just tell you it does not meet our current needs, but a simple rejection letter would not convey our astonishment that you would even offer this work for publication.

Simply put, Mr. Arbuthnot, your plot is too bizarre for even the most outré fiction. Two presidential candidates battle to a tie so close that a handful of sunbelt retirees hold the fate of the world in their hands? The electoral process thrown into the courts? And one candidate's brother is governor of the critical state? Come on, Mr. Arbuthnot! What reader is going to know what "dimpled chad" is, anyway?

A political thriller may be wildly imaginative, sir, but it must be at least marginally plausible. We suggest a career other than writing... Perhaps sheepherding or hotel-motel management.

BEN SARGENT
Courtesy Austin American-Statesman

SCOTT STANTIS
Courtesy Birmingham News

18

"Frankly, I'm surprised you've managed to keep it running as long as you have..."

DAVE GRANLUND
Courtesy Metrowest Daily News (Mass.)

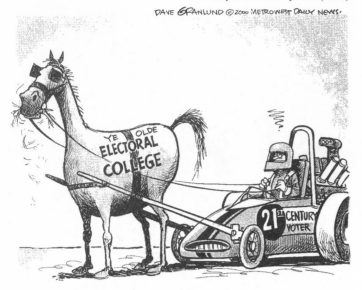

MARSHALL RAMSEY
Courtesy Jackson Clarion-Ledger (Miss.)

# EVERY VOTE COUNTS... EXCEPT IN PALM BEACH COUNTY?

email: pamwinters@email.com

PAM WINTERS
Courtesy San Diego Union-Tribune

DREW SHENEMAN
Courtesy Newark Star-Ledger

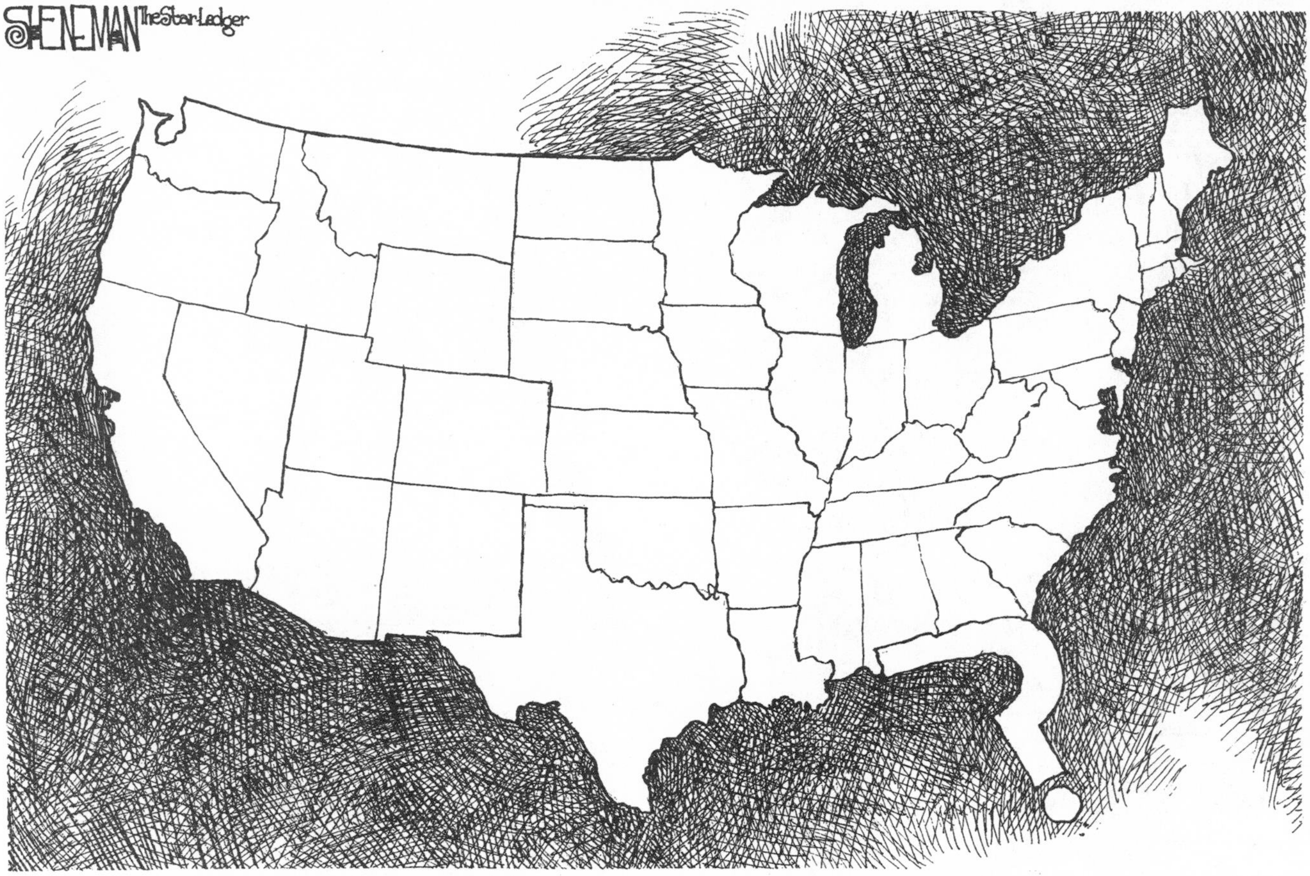
SHENEMAN The Star-Ledger

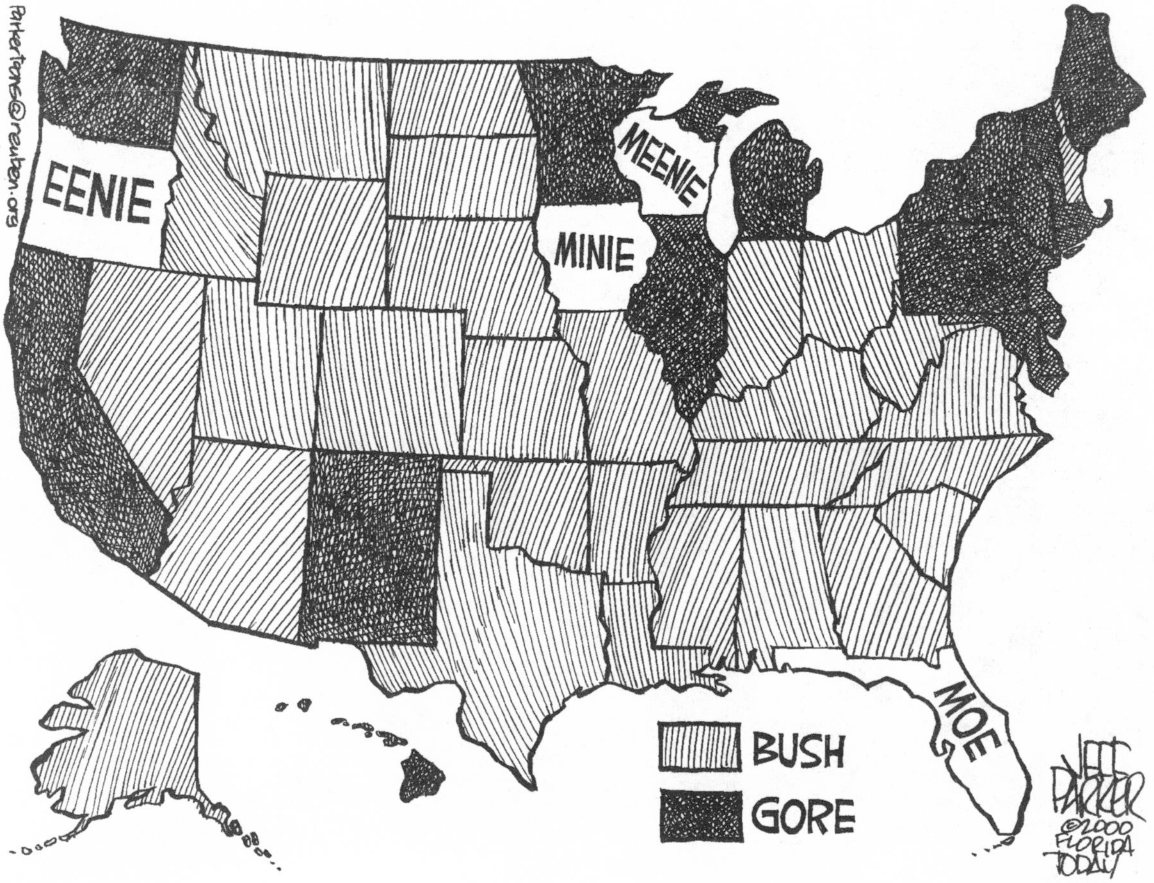
ParkerToons@reuben.org
EENIE
MEENIE
MINIE
MOE
BUSH
GORE
JEFF PARKER ©2000 FLORIDA TODAY

JEFF PARKER
Courtesy Florida Today

ROBERT ARIAIL
Courtesy The State (S.C.)

DICK LOCHER
Courtesy Chicago Tribune

MARGULIES
©2000 THE RECORD NEW JERSEY
www.bergen.com/margulies

JIMMY MARGULIES
Courtesy Hackensack Record

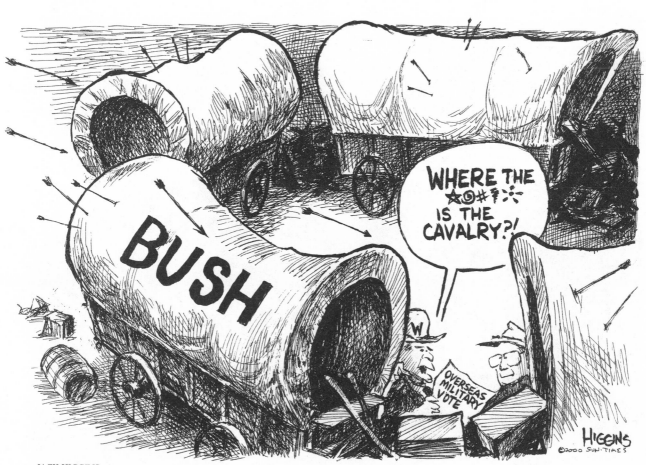

JACK HIGGINS
Courtesy Chicago Sun-Times

JOHN SHERFFIUS
Courtesy St. Louis Post-Dispatch

**The hanging chad**

STEVE WETZEL
Courtesy Harrisburg Patriot-News

WHAT THIS PRESIDENTIAL ELECTION IS ALL ABOUT.

CLAY JONES
Courtesy Free Lance Star (Va.)

BRUCE QUAST
Courtesy Rockford Register-Star

MIKE RITTER
Courtesy Tribune Newspapers

DICK LOCHER
Courtesy Chicago Tribune

JEFF STAHLER
Courtesy Cincinnati Post

ANNETTE BALESTERI
Courtesy Antioch Ledger Dispatch (Calif.)

WAYNE STAYSKAL
Courtesy Tampa Tribune

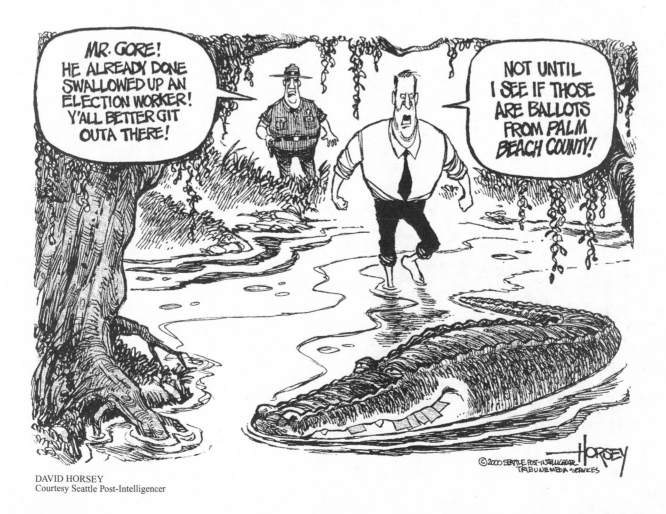

DAVID HORSEY
Courtesy Seattle Post-Intelligencer

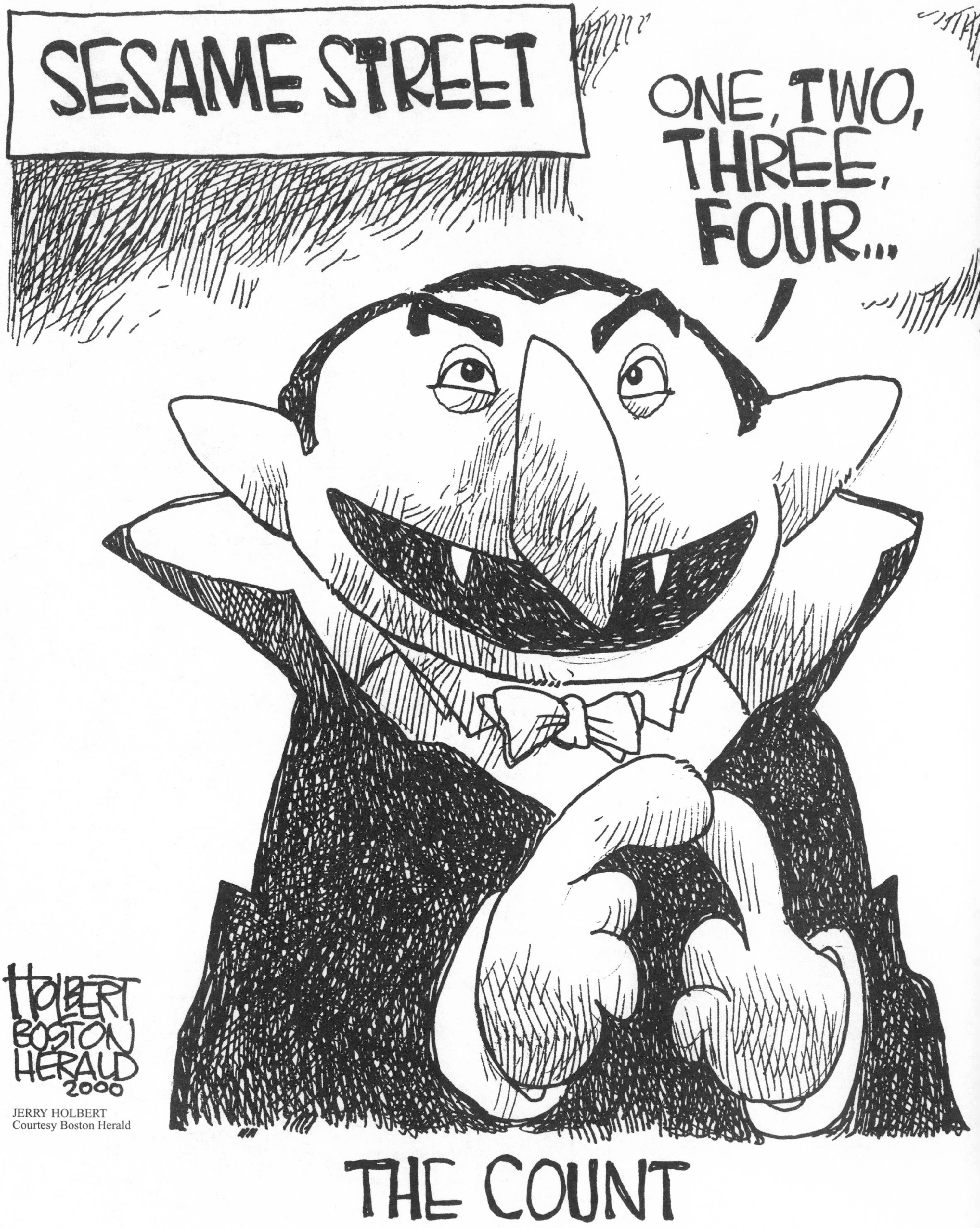

SESAME STREET
ONE, TWO, THREE, FOUR...
HOLBERT BOSTON HERALD 2000
THE COUNT


JERRY HOLBERT
Courtesy Boston Herald

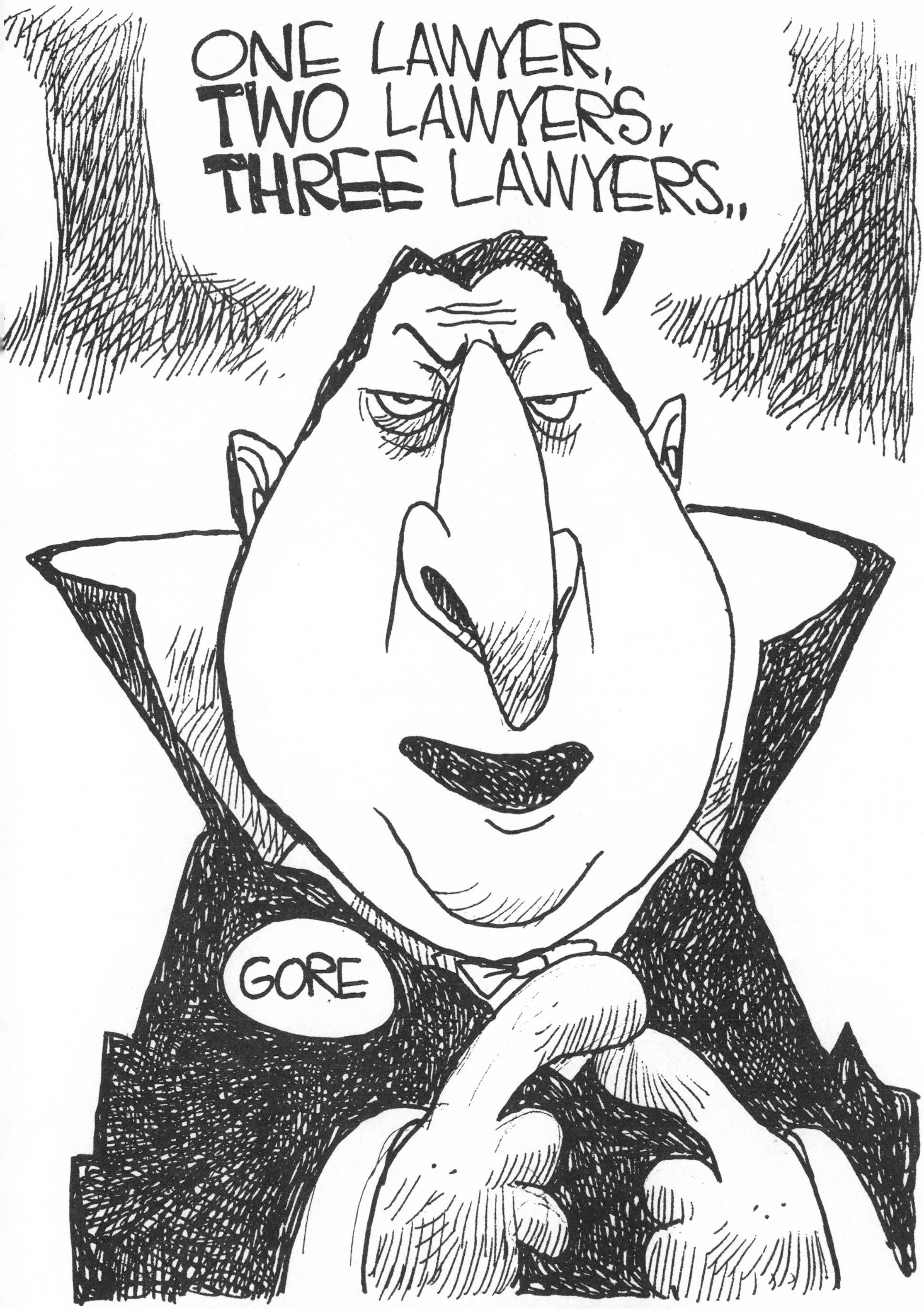
ONE LAWYER,
TWO LAWYERS,
THREE LAWYERS,,
GORE

THE RECOUNT

BILL GARNER
Courtesy Washington Times

DAVID HORSEY
Courtesy Seattle Post-Intelligencer

• THE LAWYERS DESCEND ON FLORIDA •

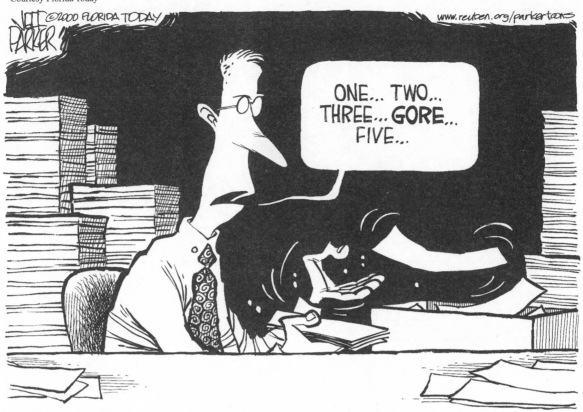

MEANWHILE... THE HAND COUNT CONTINUES IN FLORIDA...

ED STEIN
Courtesy Rocky Mountain News

ED GAMBLE
Courtesy Florida Times-Union

DAVE GRANLUND
Courtesy Metrowest Daily News (Mass.)

34

DOUG REGALIA
Courtesy Contra Costa Times (Calif.)

JOHN SPENCER
Courtesy Philadelphia Business Journal

JOHN BRANCH
Courtesy San Antonio Express-News

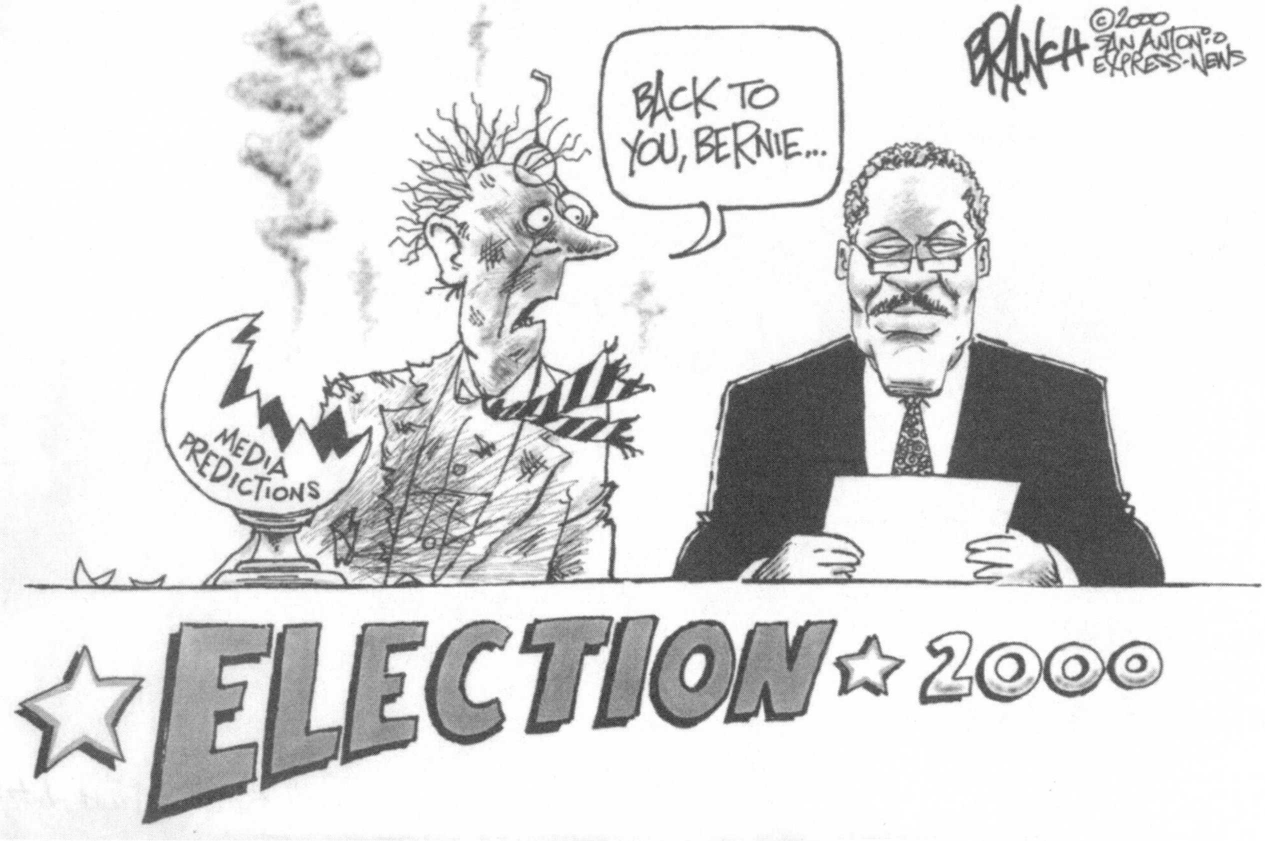
BRANCH ©2000 SAN ANTONIO EXPRESS-NEWS
BACK TO YOU, BERNIE...
MEDIA PREDICTIONS
ELECTION 2000

MIKE PETERS
Courtesy Dayton Daily News

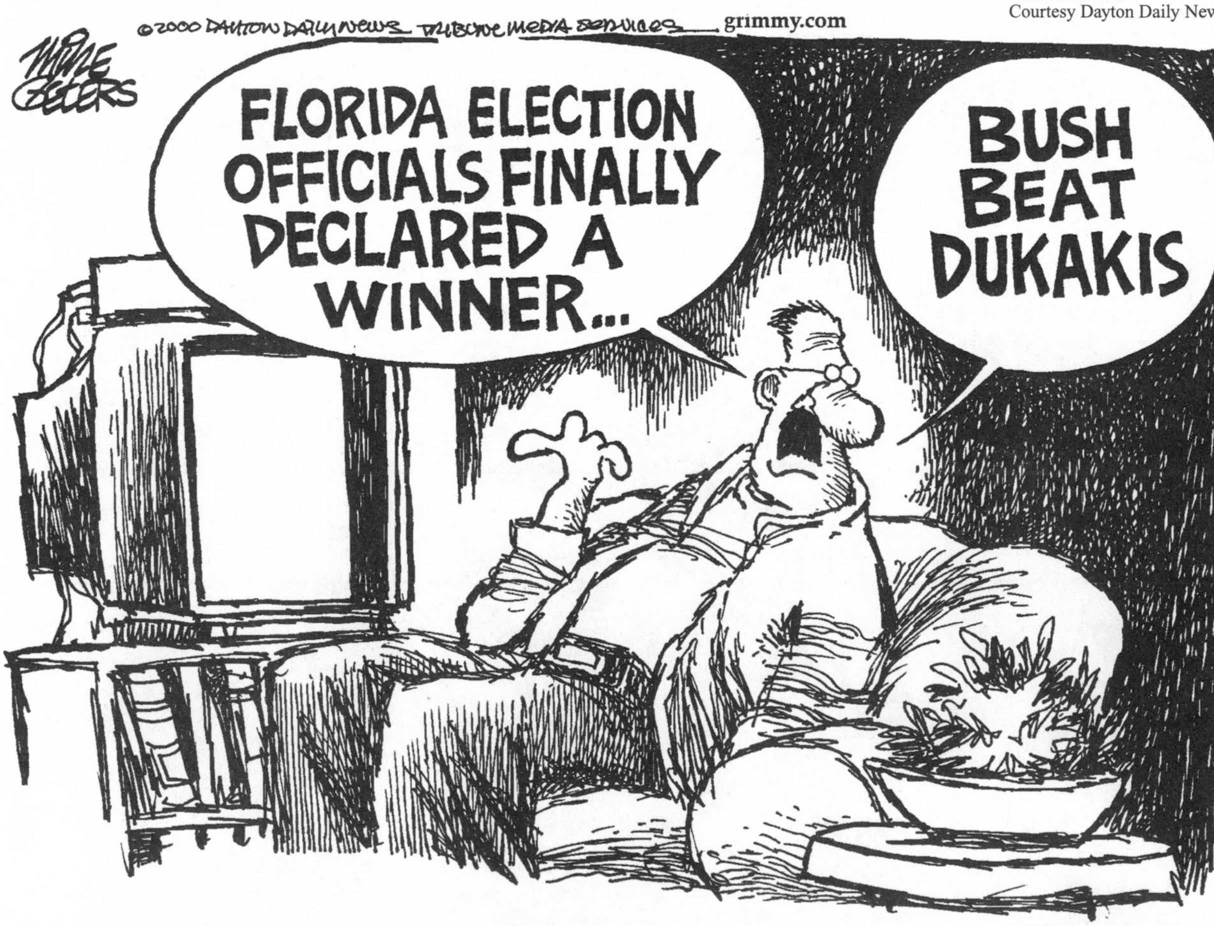
grimmy.com
MIKE PETERS
FLORIDA ELECTION OFFICIALS FINALLY DECLARED A WINNER...
BUSH BEAT DUKAKIS

JACK HIGGINS
Courtesy Chicago Sun-Times

MARK STREETER
Courtesy Savannah Morning News

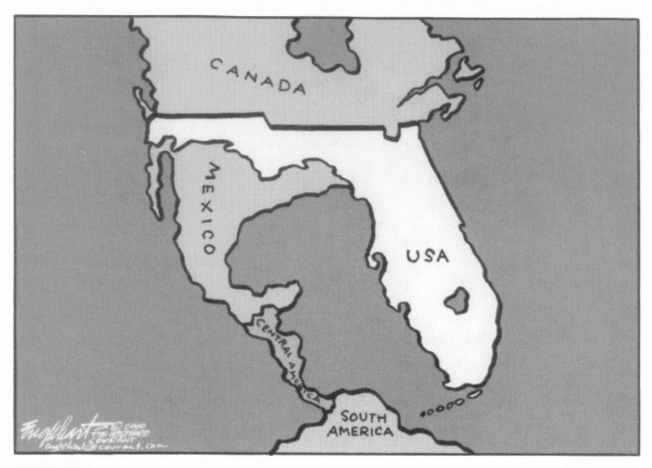

BOB ENGLEHART
Courtesy Hartford Courant

PATRICK ALAN RICE
Courtesy Jupiter Courier

ONE VOTE THAT COUNTS

"BUTTERFLY BALLOT"

www.fredmulhearn.com

TOP TEN REASONS
OUR MACHINES ARE BETTER
THAN FLORIDA'S PUNCH-CARDS

10. No hanging chads.
9. No butterfly ballots.
8. No hand counts.
7. No votes thrown out.
6. They don't attract as many lawyers.
5. You can't vote twice for the same office.
4. Don't have to discern intent of voters.
3. Re-counts are quick.
2. When it's over, you know who's won.
1. Every vote counts.

STEVE YORK
Courtesy Kankakee Daily Journal

JEFF KOTERBA
Courtesy Omaha World-Herald

# The Presidential Campaign

The 2000 U.S. presidential campaign pitted Gov. George W. Bush of Texas, the son of a former president, against Vice President Al Gore of Tennessee, the son of a former United States senator. Bush had triumphed over Sen. John McCain, a Vietnam War hero, for the Republican Party nomination, while Gore had turned back a spirited challenge by former Sen. Bill Bradley to become the Democrat's standard bearer.

The campaign seemed to turn on three televised debates, which Gore was expected to win easily because of his vast experience in Washington affairs. Bush, however, managed to hold his own. Polls showed that voters believed he won at least two of the debates while elevating himself considerably in the public's eyes. Throughout the campaign, Gore was plagued by accusations that many of his claims about personal matters and his government service were false.

The Reform Party engaged in a bitter squabble before former Republican Pat Buchanan finally was named its candidate. His campaign, however, never really got off the ground. But longtime consumer activist Ralph Nader, running as the Green Party candidate, gave Gore and the Democrats fits. His appeal was primarily to left-leaning voters who otherwise would have been expected to support the Democratic candidate. Despite a concerted effort to persuade Nader to withdraw, he refused to budge. Many observers concluded that his presence on the ballot had cost Gore the election.

EUGENE PAYNE
Courtesy Charlotte Observer

LARRY WRIGHT
Courtesy Detroit News

RICHARD CROWSON
Courtesy Wichita Eagle

ANN TELNAES
Courtesy Austin American-Statesman

# Berry's World

*"Time is running out. Instead of overnight guests, let's go to HOURLY guests."*

DAVID HITCH
Courtesy Worcester Telegram and Gazette

MIKE RITTER
Courtesy Tribune Newspapers

MICHAEL RAMIREZ
Courtesy Los Angeles Times

DREW SHENEMAN
Courtesy Newark Star-Ledger

"WELL, WE FAILED TO SECURE FEDERAL FUNDS, THREW THE RACE INTO TURMOIL, AND POSSIBLY GAVE THE ELECTION TO A TEXAS OIL BARON. WHAT SHOULD WE DO FOR AN ENCORE, CLUB A BABY SEAL?"

VIC HARVILLE
Courtesy Donrey News (Ark.)

KEN DAVIS
Courtesy Cedartown Standard (Ga.)

MARK THORNHILL
Courtesy North County Times (Calif.)

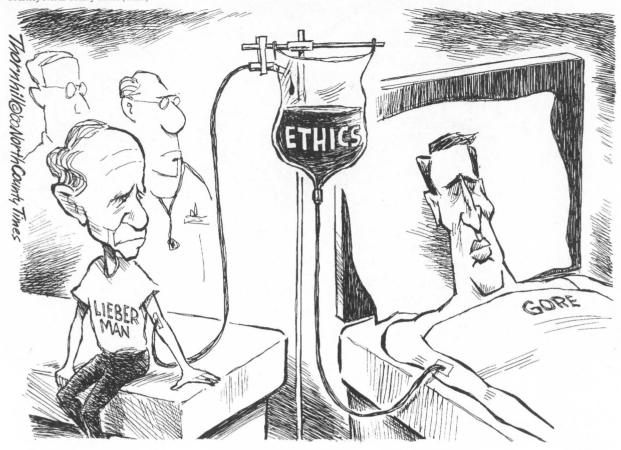

SCOTT STANTIS
Courtesy Birmingham News

47

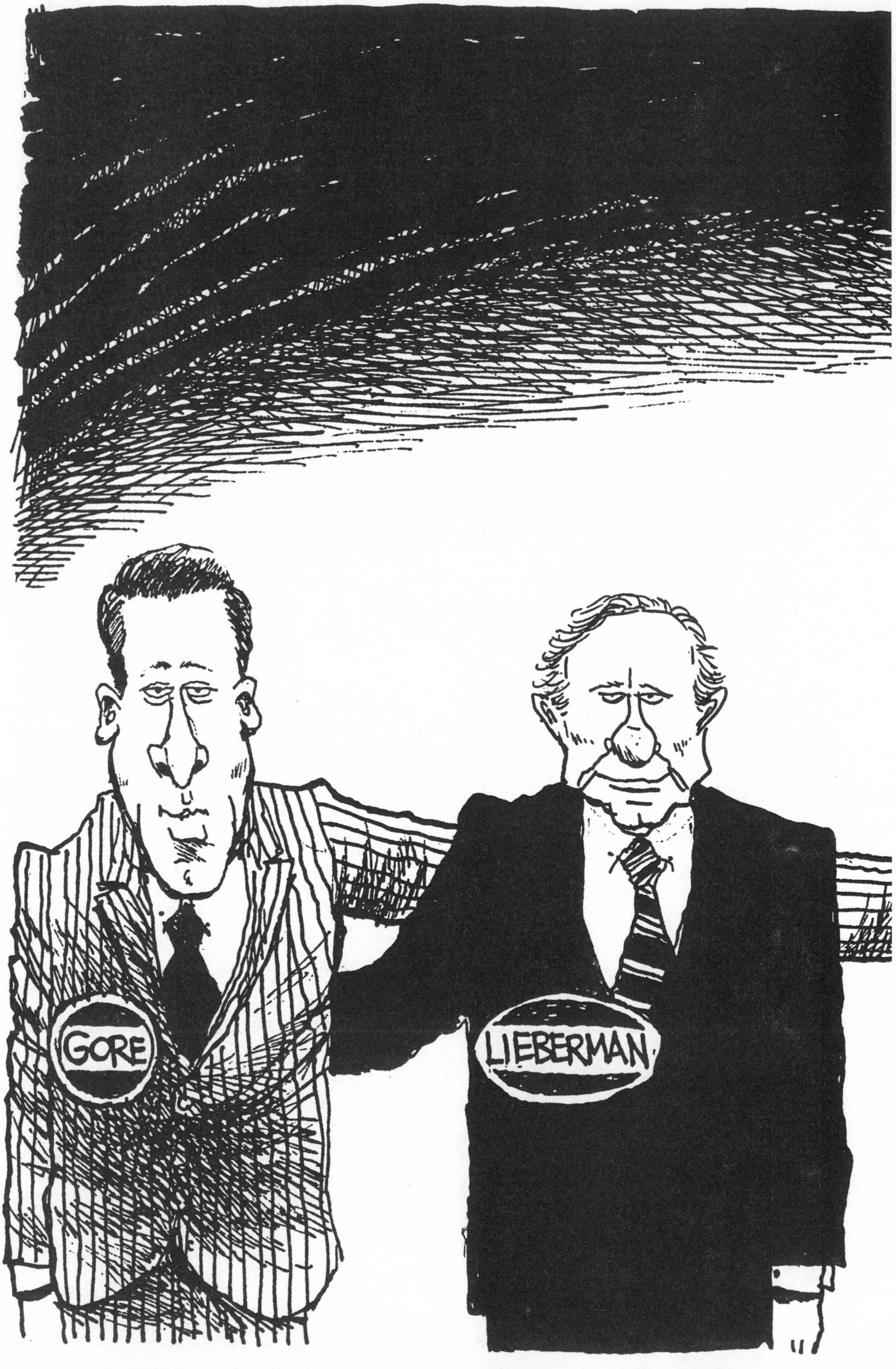
GORE
LIEBERMAN

GARY MARKSTEIN
Courtesy Milwaukee Journal Sentinel

JOE HELLER
Courtesy Green Bay Press-Gazette

TIM HARTMAN
Courtesy The Valley News (Pa.)

STEVE GREENBERG
Courtesy Jewish Bulletin

TIM HARTMAN
Courtesy The Valley News (Pa.)

DAVID HORSEY
Courtesy Seattle Post-Intelligencer

MIKE PETERS
Courtesy Dayton Daily News

THEY WALK THE STREETS, DOOMED TO LIVES OF UNCERTAINTY. FOREVER DESTINED TO WANDER AIMLESSLY. THEY ARE...

# THE UNDECIDED

DREW SHENEMAN
Courtesy Newark Star-Ledger

VIC CANTONE
Courtesy Brooklyn Paper Publications

KEVIN KALLAUGHER
Courtesy Baltimore Sun

RICHARD WALLMEYER
Courtesy Long Beach Press Telegram

PAUL CONRAD
Courtesy Los Angeles Times

ROB CHAMBERS
Courtesy The Signal (Calif.)

CHARLES DANIEL
Courtesy Knoxville News-Sentinel

GARY MARKSTEIN
Courtesy Milwaukee Journal Sentinel

CAMPAIGN DEBATE

POLYGRAPH

THE CHRISTIAN SCIENCE MONITOR

CLAY BENNETT
Courtesy Christian Science Monitor

JOHN SHERFFIUS
Courtesy St. Louis Post-Dispatch

56

RICK KOLLINGER
Courtesy Easton Star-Democrat (Md.)

BEN SARGENT
Courtesy Austin American-Statesman

TIM GIBB
Courtesy Tribune-Democrat

DARYL CAGLE
Courtesy Midweek (Hawaii)

REX BABIN
Courtesy Sacramento Bee

WALT HANDELSMAN
Courtesy New Orleans Times-Picayune

MIKE PETERS
Courtesy Dayton Daily News

CLAY JONES
Courtesy Free Lance Star (Va.)

CHIP BECK
Courtesy The Real Washington

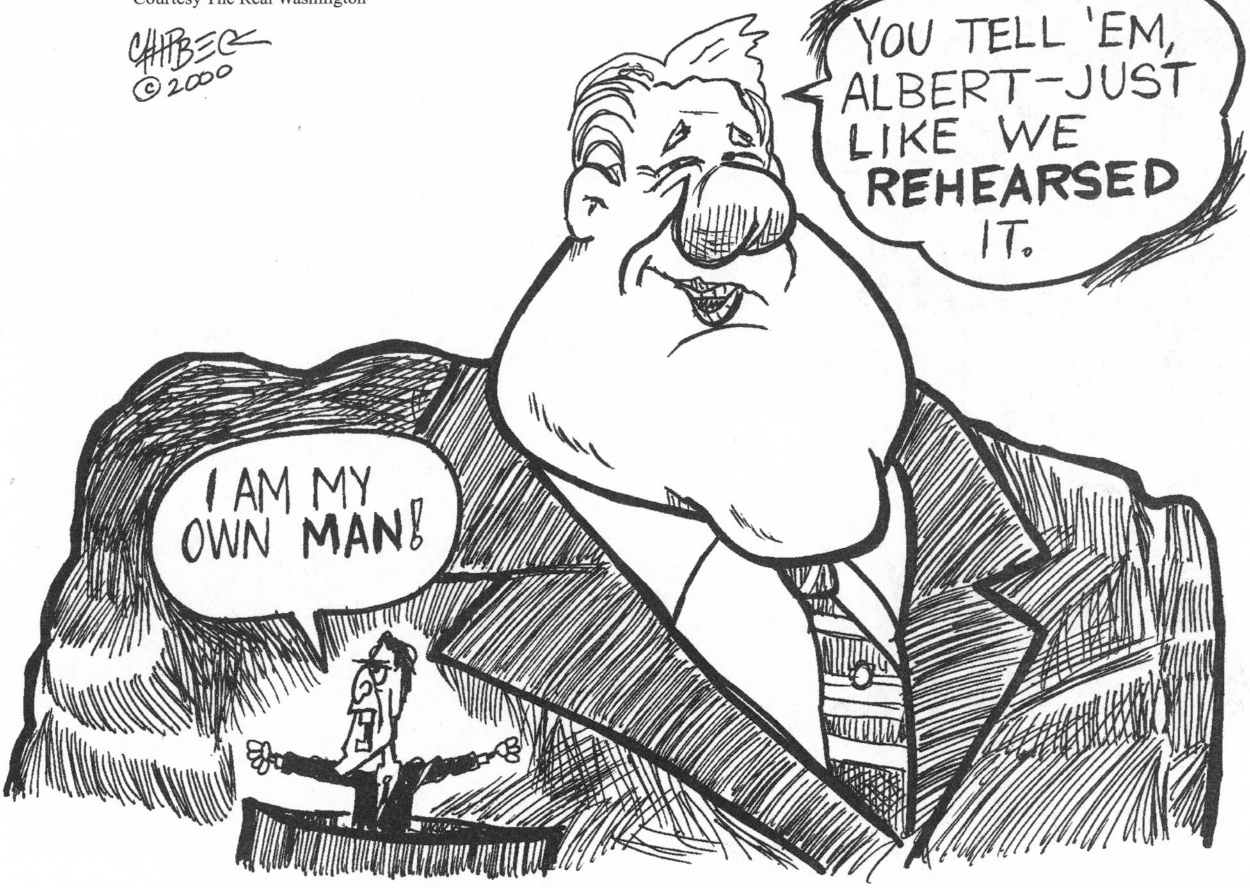

CHIPBECK ©2000
YOU TELL 'EM, ALBERT—JUST LIKE WE REHEARSED IT.
I AM MY OWN MAN!


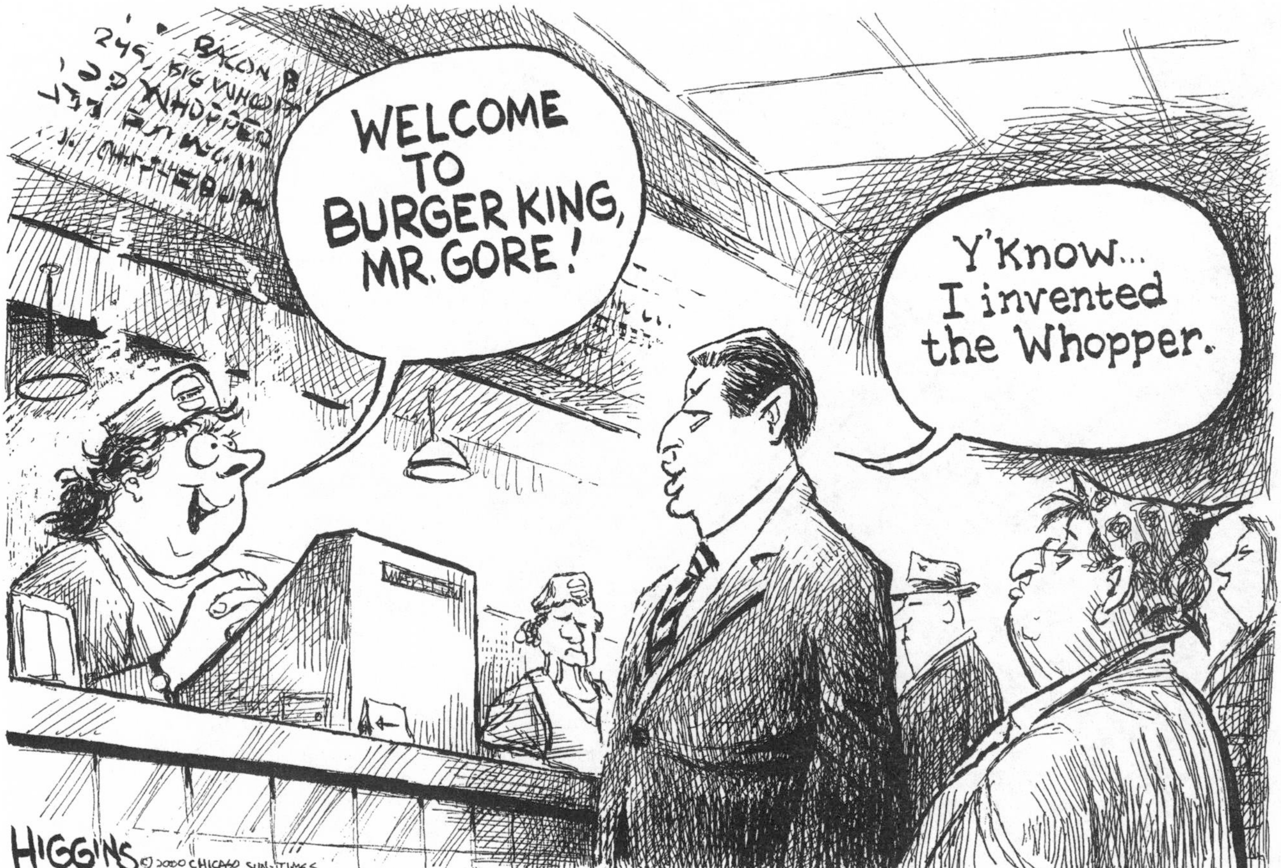

WELCOME TO BURGER KING, MR. GORE!
Y'Know... I invented the Whopper.
HIGGINS © 2000 CHICAGO SUN-TIMES


JACK HIGGINS
Courtesy Chicago Sun-Times

LAZARO FRESQUET
Courtesy El Nuevo Herald (Miami)

RICK KOLLINGER
Courtesy Easton Star-Democrat (Md.)

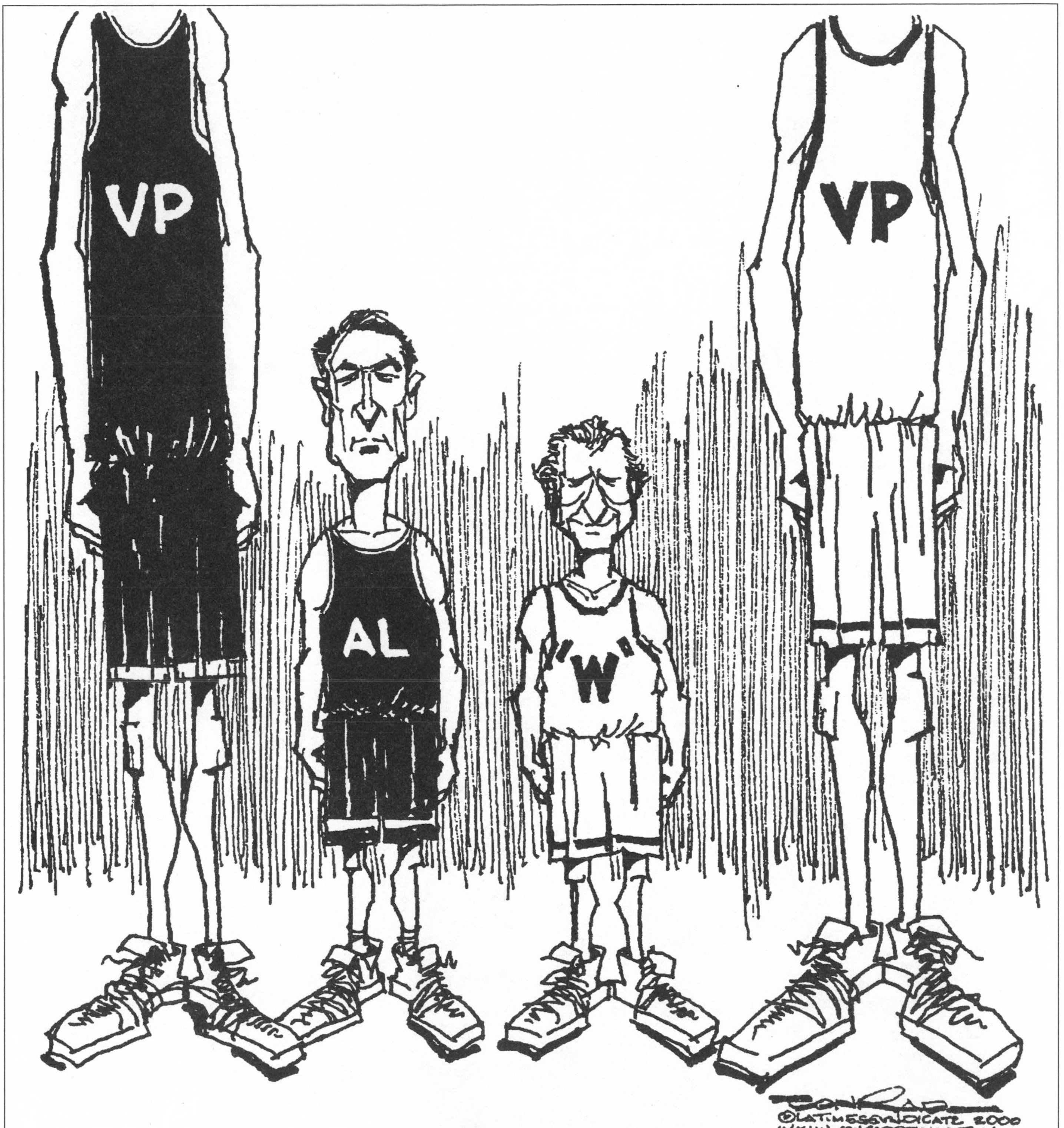
VP
AL
"W"
VP
CONRAD
©LATIMESSYNDICATE 2000
WWW.CONRADPROJECTS.COM
THE FINAL FOUR

PAUL CONRAD
Courtesy Los Angeles Times

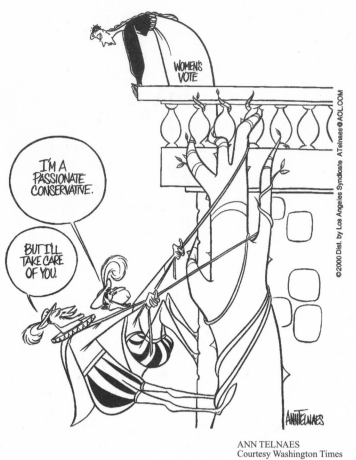

ANN TELNAES
Courtesy Washington Times

REX BABIN
Courtesy Sacramento Bee

S. C. RAWLS
Courtesy NEA

GARY VARVEL
Courtesy Indianapolis Star

STEPHEN TEMPLETON
Courtesy Fayetteville Observer-Times (N.C.)

BOB ENGLEHART
Courtesy Hartford Courant

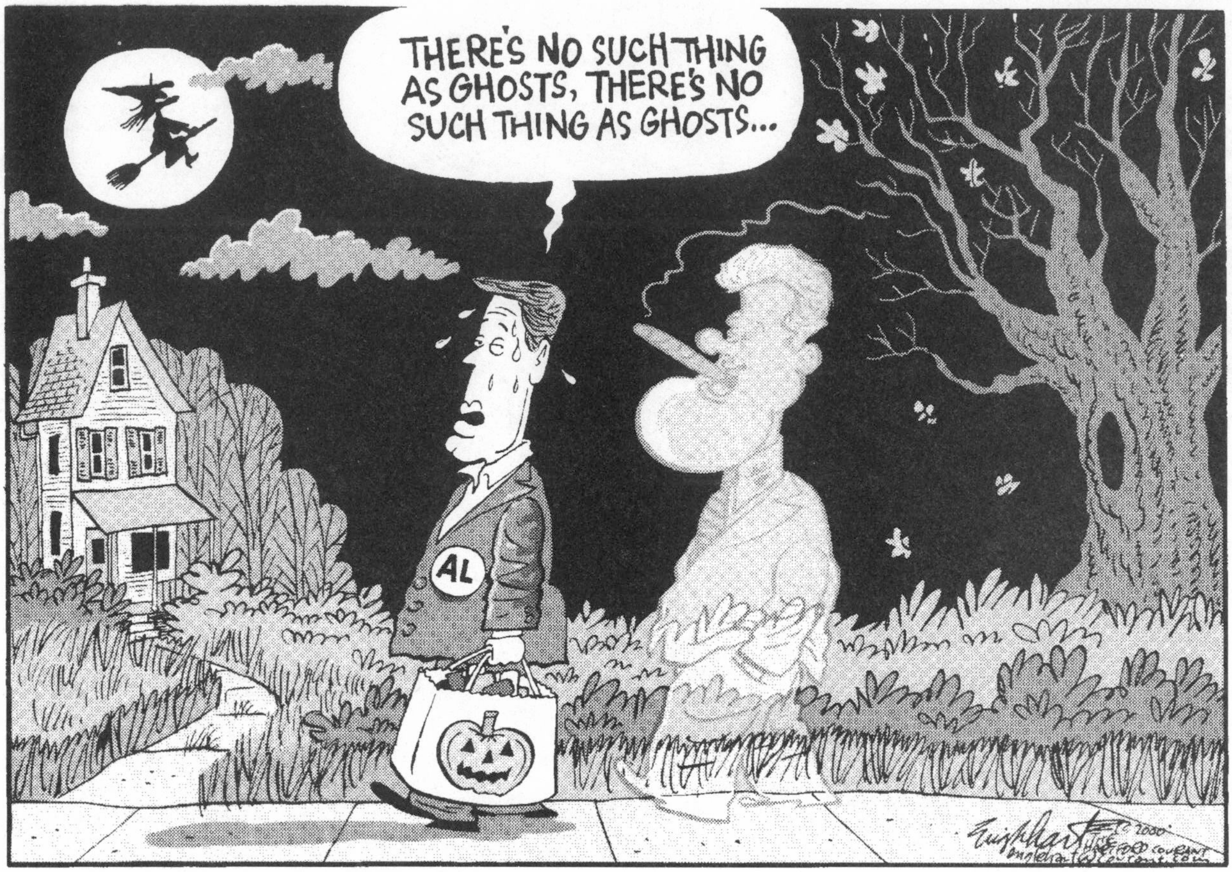
THERE'S NO SUCH THING AS GHOSTS, THERE'S NO SUCH THING AS GHOSTS...
AL

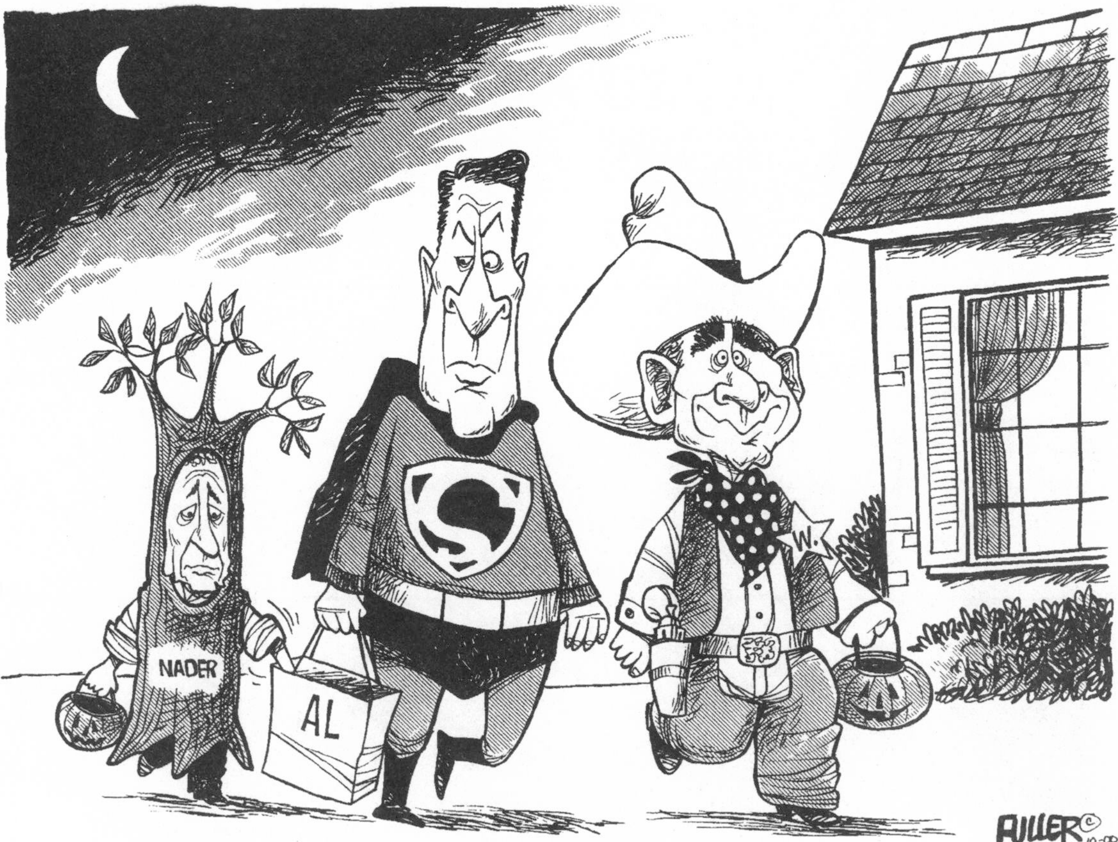
NADER
AL
W.
FULLER © 10-00 THE GAINESVILLE SUN

JAKE FULLER
Courtesy Gainesville Sun

ROBERT ARIAIL
Courtesy The State (S.C.)

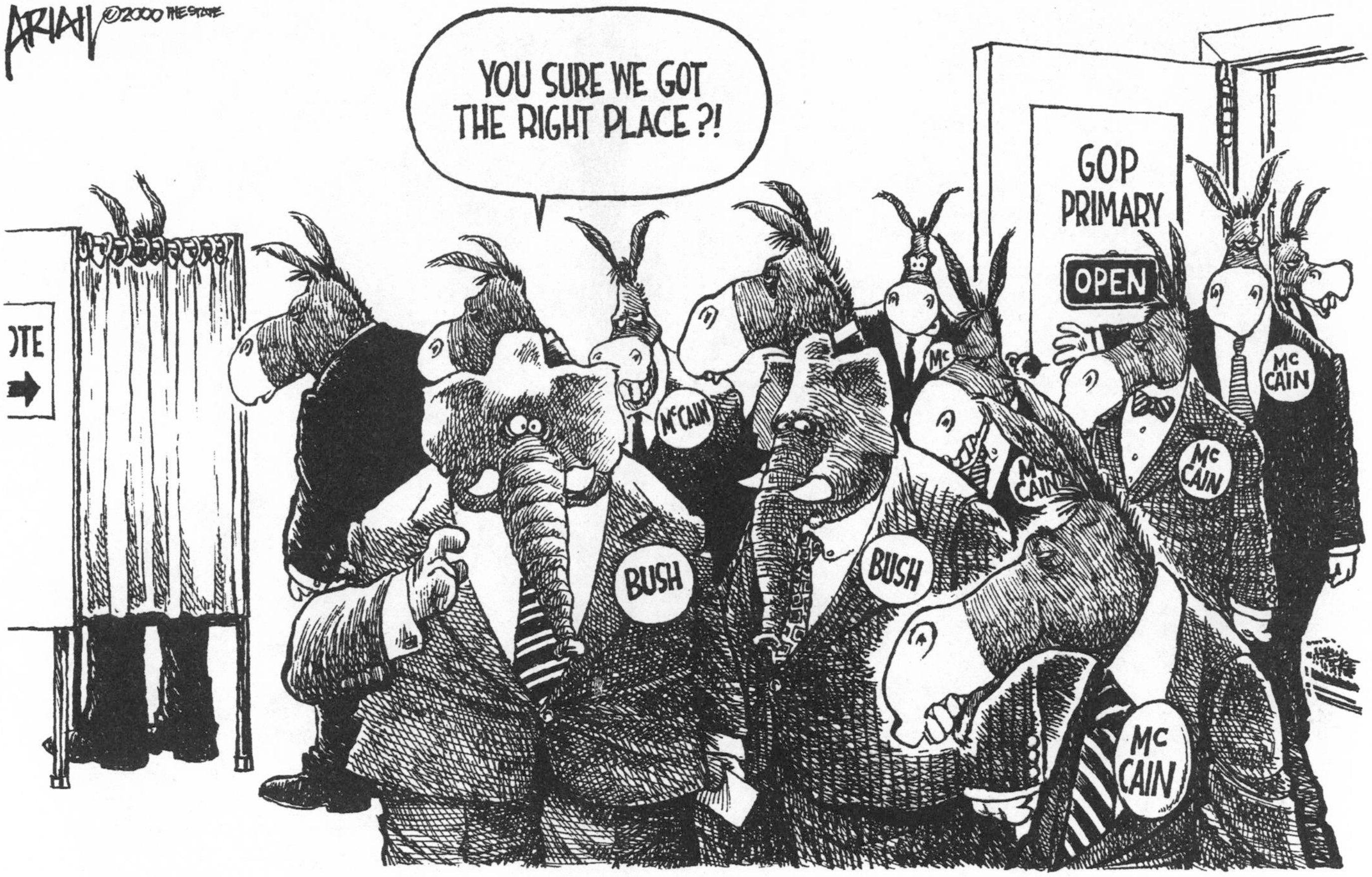
ARIAIL ©2000 THE STATE
YOU SURE WE GOT THE RIGHT PLACE ?!
GOP PRIMARY
OPEN
BUSH
BUSH
McCAIN
McCAIN
McCAIN
McCAIN
McCAIN
Mc

SCOTT STANTIS
Courtesy Birmingham News

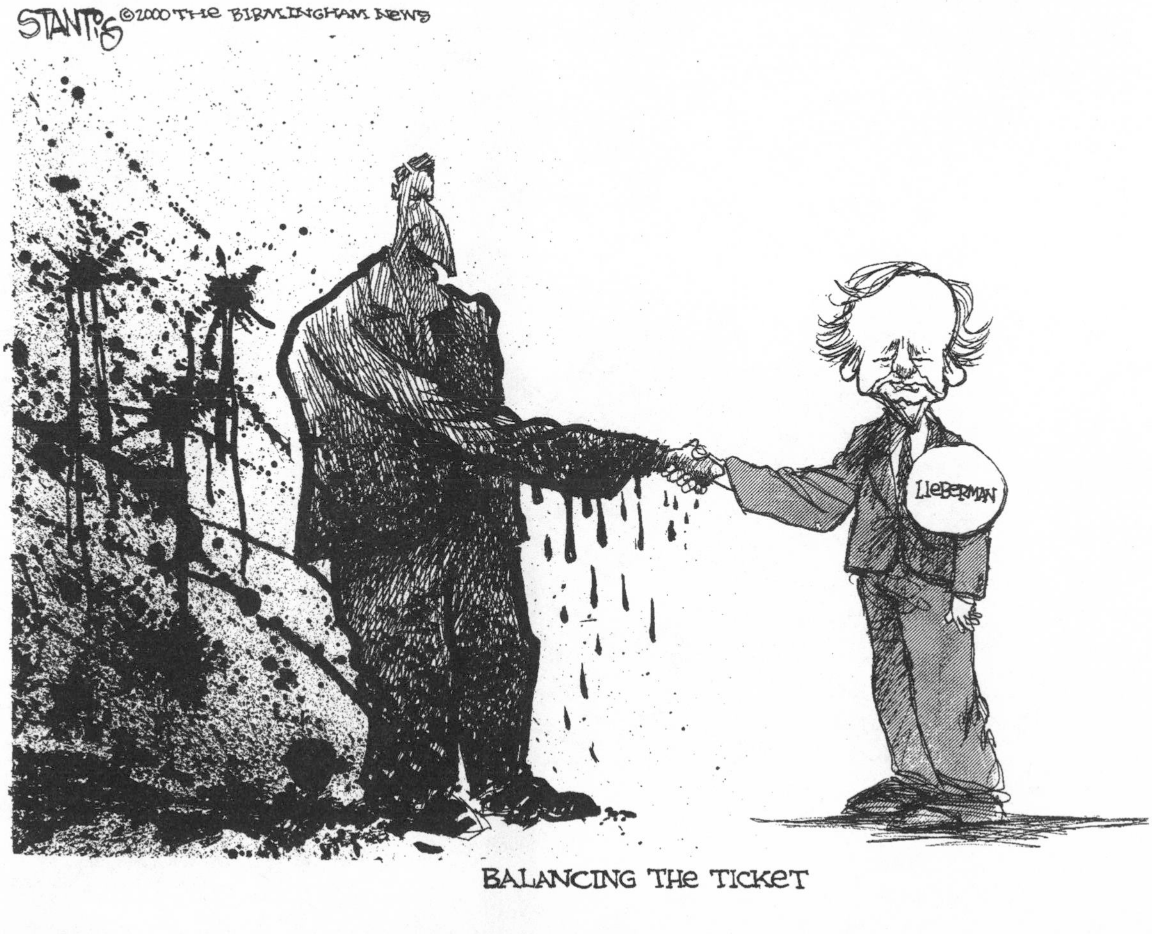
STANTIS ©2000 THE BIRMINGHAM NEWS
LIEBERMAN

BALANCING THE TICKET

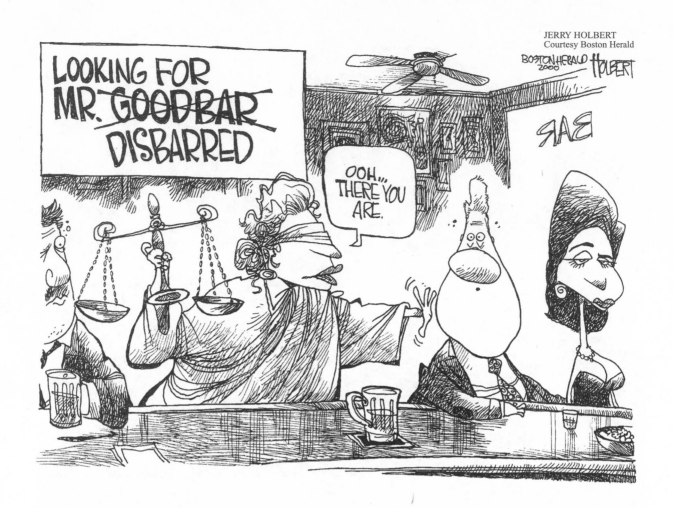

JERRY HOLBERT
Courtesy Boston Herald

FRANK CAMMUSO
Courtesy Syracuse Herald-Journal

# The Clinton Administration

Atty. Gen. Janet Reno and the U.S. Justice Department argued in federal court that Microsoft's Windows monopoly gave it far too much power, and a judge ordered that Bill Gates' company be split in two. Years of legal wrangling, however, lie ahead before all appeals are completed. Reno also ordered a S.W.A.T. team to snatch six-year-old Elian Gonzalez from the Miami home of relatives and return him to Cuba.

Secret information about nuclear weapons disappeared from the Los Alamos laboratory in New Mexico. Coming in the wake of other sensitive information having been sold to and stolen by China, the incident refocused attention on the Clinton Administration's failure to protect the nation's secrets.

President Clinton worked feverishly throughout the year to create an enduring legacy that would overshadow his impeachment, his much-trumpeted dalliance with Monica Lewinsky, and the other scandals surrounding his administration. He traveled more than any other president, visiting California 56 times, hosted 200 fundraisers in 2000 alone, and traveled to 54 foreign countries. He labored long and hard in search of a peace agreement in the Middle East. But no real progress was made toward shoring up his shaky legacy.

MICHAEL RAMIREZ
Courtesy Los Angeles Times

CLINTON'S LEGACY

FRED CURATOLO
Courtesy Edmonton Sun

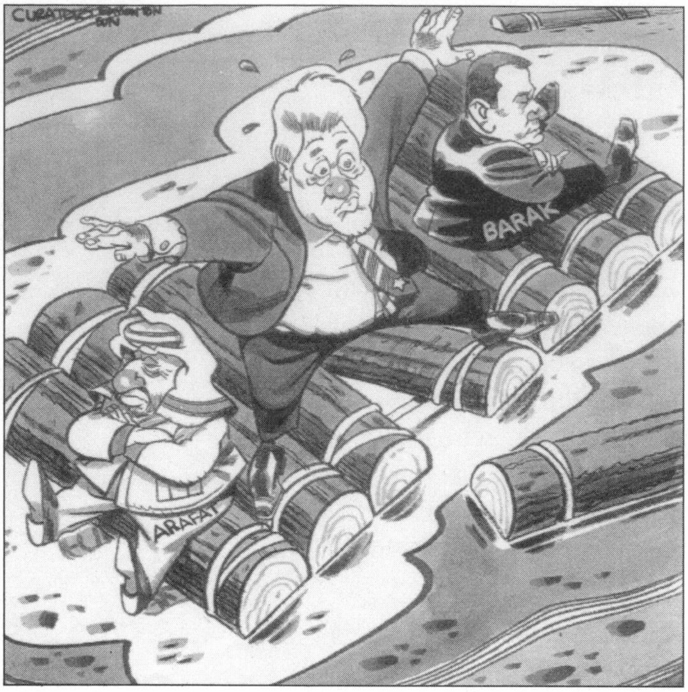
BARAK
ARAFAT

TOM BECK
Courtesy Freeport Journal-Standard (Ill.)

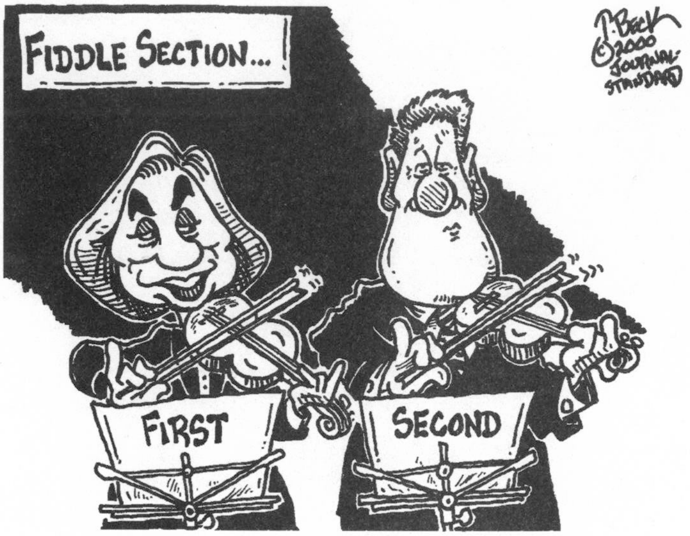
FIDDLE SECTION...
FIRST
SECOND

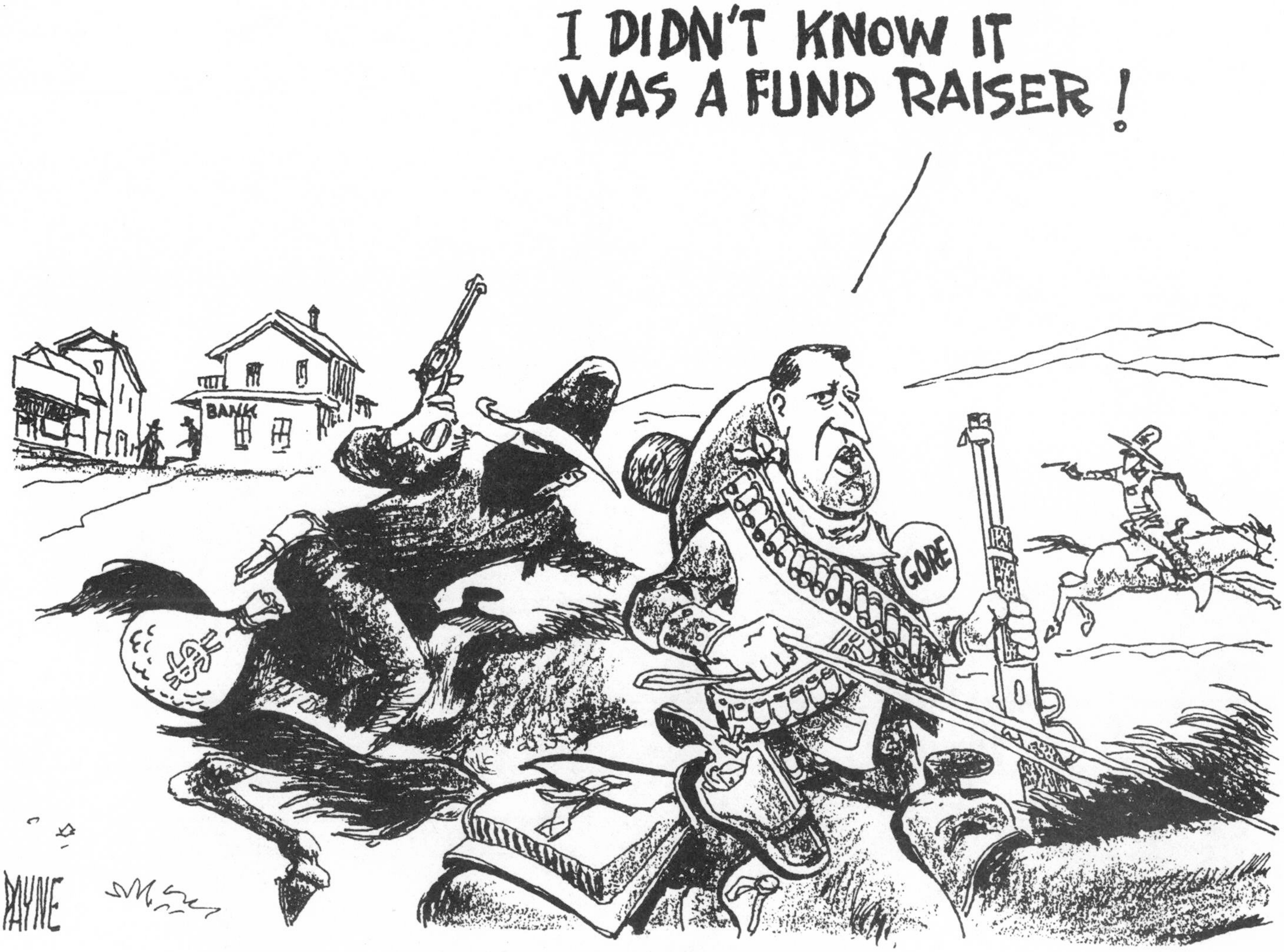
I DIDN'T KNOW IT WAS A FUND RAISER!
BANK
GORE
PAYNE

EUGENE PAYNE
Courtesy Charlotte Observer

SCOTT STANTIS
Courtesy Birmingham News

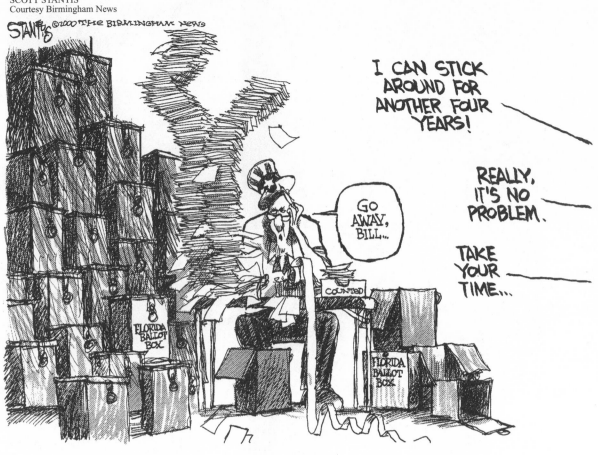

GLENN MCCOY
Courtesy Belleville News-Democrat (Ill.)

J. R. ROSE
Courtesy Byrd Newspapers

JACK JURDEN
Courtesy Wilmington News Journal

SCOTT STANTIS
Courtesy Birmingham News

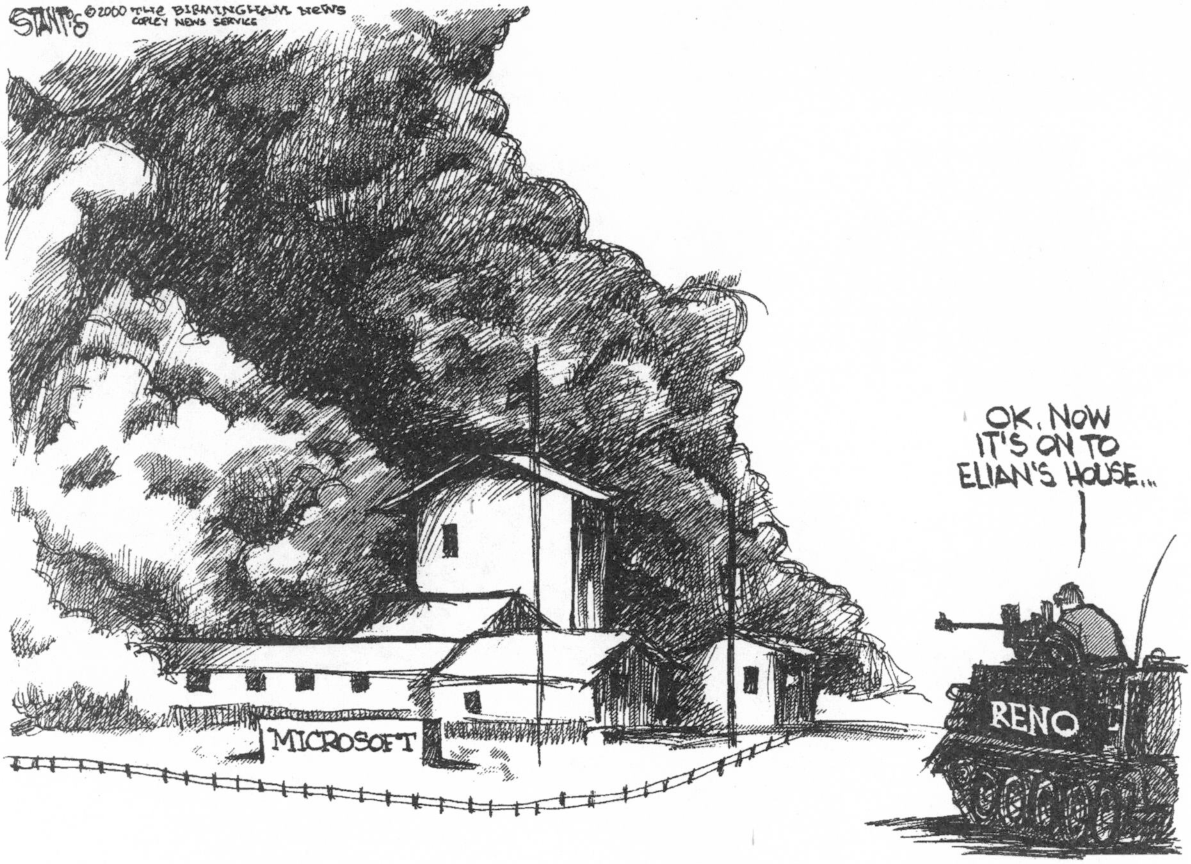
STANTIS ©2000 THE BIRMINGHAM NEWS COPLEY NEWS SERVICE
OK. NOW IT'S ON TO ELIAN'S HOUSE...
RENO
MICROSOFT

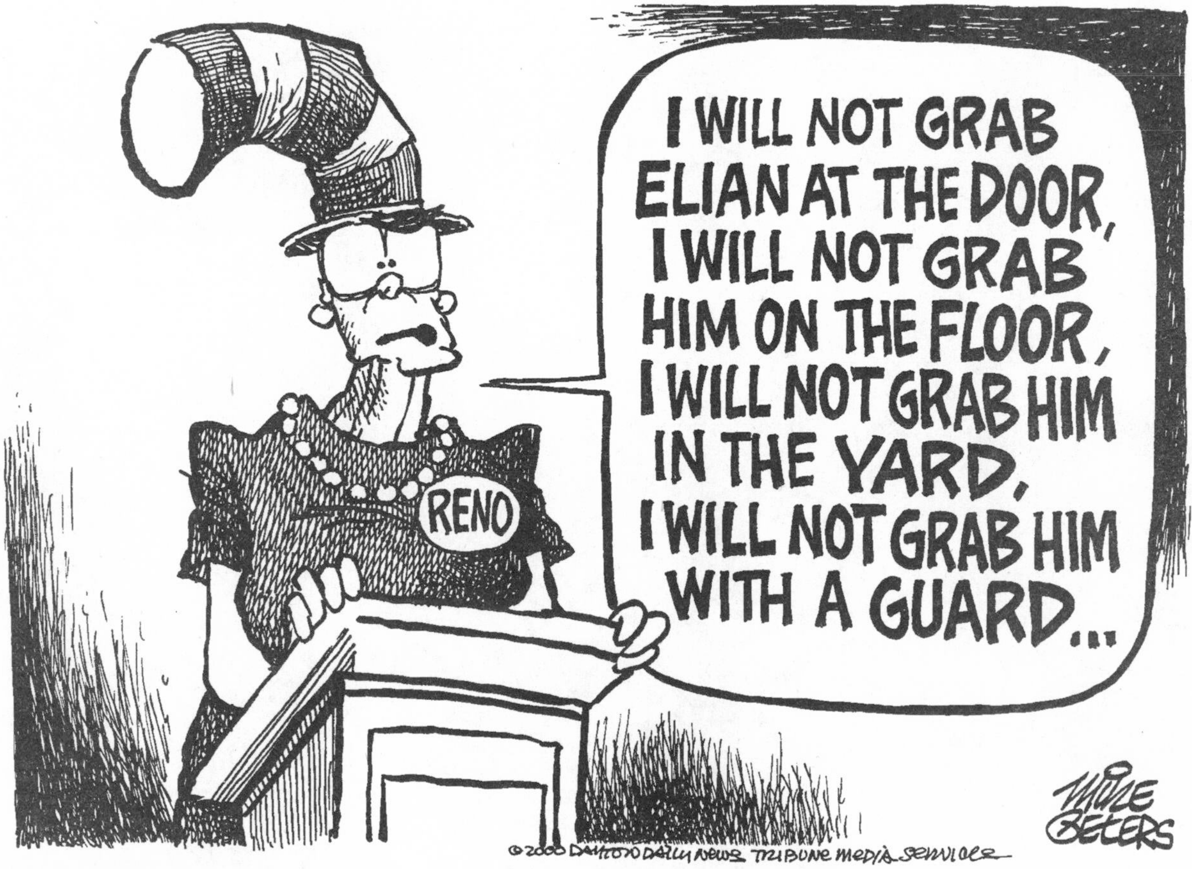
I WILL NOT GRAB ELIAN AT THE DOOR, I WILL NOT GRAB HIM ON THE FLOOR, I WILL NOT GRAB HIM IN THE YARD, I WILL NOT GRAB HIM WITH A GUARD...
RENO
©2000 DAYTON DAILY NEWS TRIBUNE MEDIA SERVICES
MIKE PETERS

MIKE PETERS
Courtesy Dayton Daily News

Berry's World

YOU'RE **RUINING** MY LEGACY.

www.comics.com
© 2000 by NEA, Inc.

JIM BERRY
Courtesy NEA

MARK THORNHILL
Courtesy North County Times (Calif.)

Atto-
Attorney General Reno

Atto- General Reno

General Reno

DICK LOCHER
Courtesy Chicago Tribune

WAIT! DO I HEAR A CEASE-FIRE? IS MY PEACE PROCESS WORKING?

I THINK YOU'RE HEARING THE RELOADING PROCESS.

MIDEAST

ALBRIGHT

MICHAEL THOMPSON
Courtesy Detroit Free Press

JOE HELLER
Courtesy Green Bay Press-Gazette

JIM BORGMAN
Courtesy Cincinnati Enquirer

THE BREAKUP OF MICROSOFT

BOB GORRELL
Courtesy Creators Syndicate

"SORRY . . . I CAN'T SEEM TO FIND YOU ON OUR LIST OF QUALIFIED DONORS."

JEFF MACNELLY
Courtesy Chicago Tribune

JACK HIGGINS
Courtesy Chicago Sun-Times

## Berry's World

**Al Gore gets into the spotlight**

JIM BERRY
Courtesy NEA

BILL GARNER
Courtesy Washington Times

NICK ANDERSON
Courtesy Louisville Courier-Journal

ED FISCHER
Courtesy Rochester Post-Bulletin

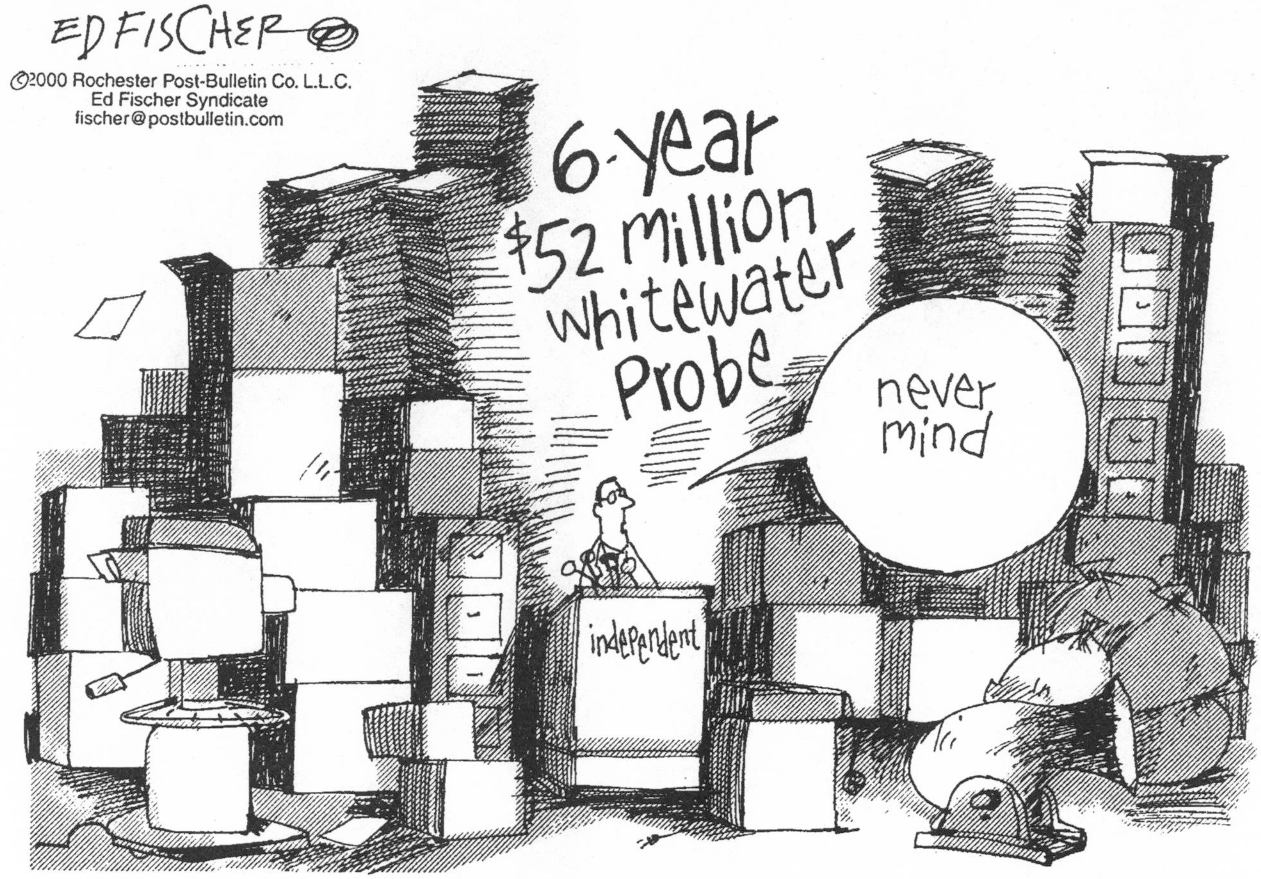
ED FISCHER
©2000 Rochester Post-Bulletin Co. L.L.C.
Ed Fischer Syndicate
fischer@postbulletin.com
6-year $52 million whitewater Probe
never mind
independent

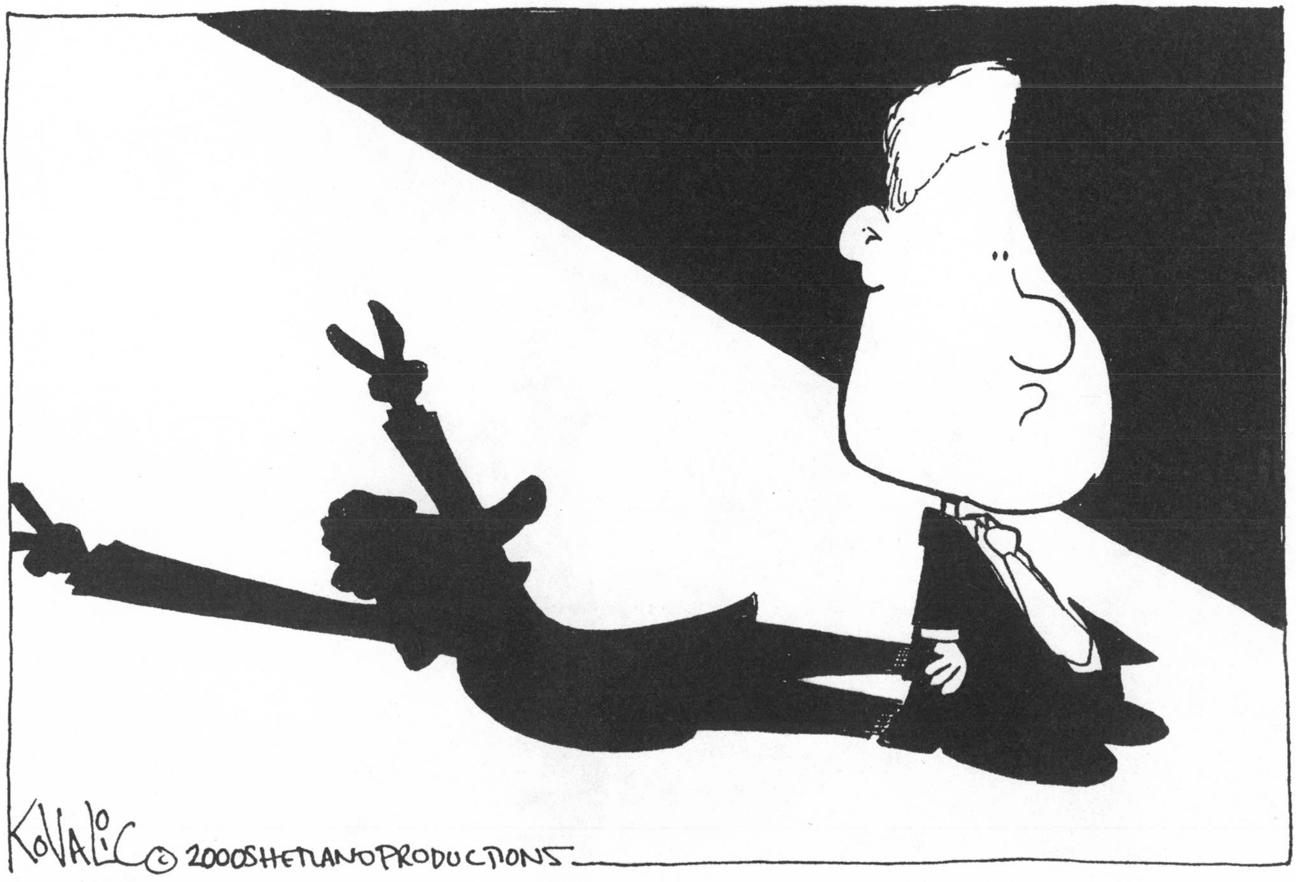
KOVALIC © 2000 SHETLAND PRODUCTIONS

JOHN KOVALIC
Courtesy Wisconsin State Journal

ARE YOU BETTER OFF NOW THAN YOU WERE EIGHT YEARS AGO?

ED HALL
Courtesy Baker County Press (Fla.)

BILL MANGOLD
Courtesy Heritage Newspapers

DALE STEPHANOS
Courtesy Boston Herald

GLENN MCCOY
Courtesy Belleville News-Democrat (Ill.)

HANK MCCLURE
Courtesy Lawton Constitution

WE'VE COME A LONG WAY, BABY.

CHAN LOWE
Courtesy Fort Lauderdale News/Sun Sentinel

JIM BUSH
Courtesy Providence Journal

ROBERT ARIAIL
Courtesy The State (S.C.)

# Foreign Affairs

Suffering from failing health for many months, Russian leader Boris Yeltsin resigned after naming Vladimir Putin as his successor. Putin subsequently won election as president in a continuing era of severe psychological and economic depression that has wracked the country.

Six-year-old Elian Gonzalez became an international celebrity after his mother and others drowned while attempting to flee from Cuba. The youngster was rescued at sea and brought to Miami, where relatives lived. His father—and Fidel Castro—demanded that he be returned, and an international tug of war ensued. After a lengthy standoff, the U.S. Justice Department forcibly took the boy from relatives and returned him to Cuba.

In Yugoslavia, strongman President Slobodan Milosevic was ousted by Vojislav Kostunica in a surprising election. At first, Milosevic refused to step down, but after 13 years of repressive rule he was hard pressed to find support, and he conceded defeat.

The Russian nuclear submarine *Kursk* sank to the bottom of the Barents Sea after an apparent explosion. All 118 of its crewmen perished. The nine-year war in Sierra Leone continued unabated, and Israel transferred virtually all of Gaza and half of the West Bank to Palestinian control.

JEFF MACNELLY
Courtesy Chicago Tribune

BRUCE BEATTIE
Courtesy Daytona Beach News-Journal

"This table is made from trees that were planted to commemorate the start of the peace process."

STEVE MCBRIDE
Courtesy Independence Daily Reporter (Kan.)

BILL MANGOLD
Courtesy Heritage Newspapers

KEVIN KALLAUGHER
Courtesy Baltimore Sun

LINDA BOILEAU
Courtesy Frankfort State Journal

STEVE NEASE
Courtesy Niagara Falls Review

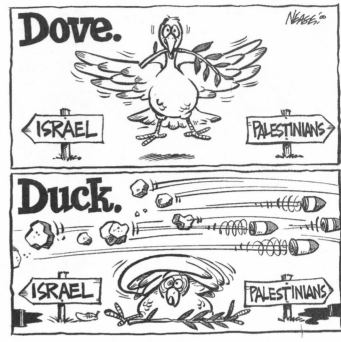

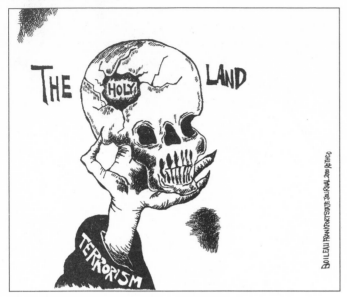

FRED CURATOLO
Courtesy Edmonton Sun

DARYL CAGLE
Courtesy Midweek (Hawaii)

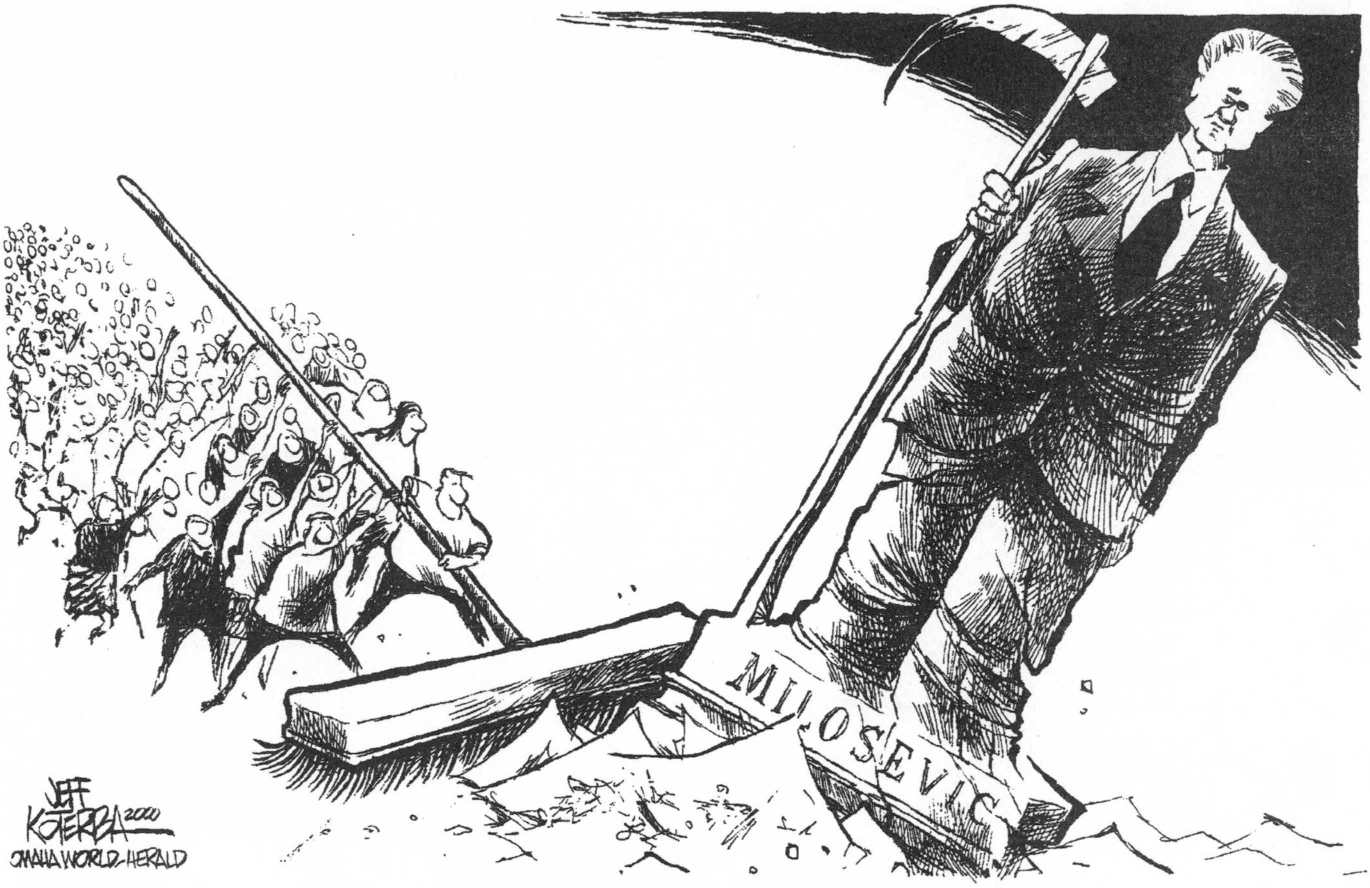
MILOSEVIC
JEFF KOTERBA 2000
OMAHA WORLD-HERALD

JEFF KOTERBA
Courtesy Omaha World-Herald

ELECTORAL CLEANSING

JOHN SHERFFIUS
Courtesy St. Louis Post-Dispatch

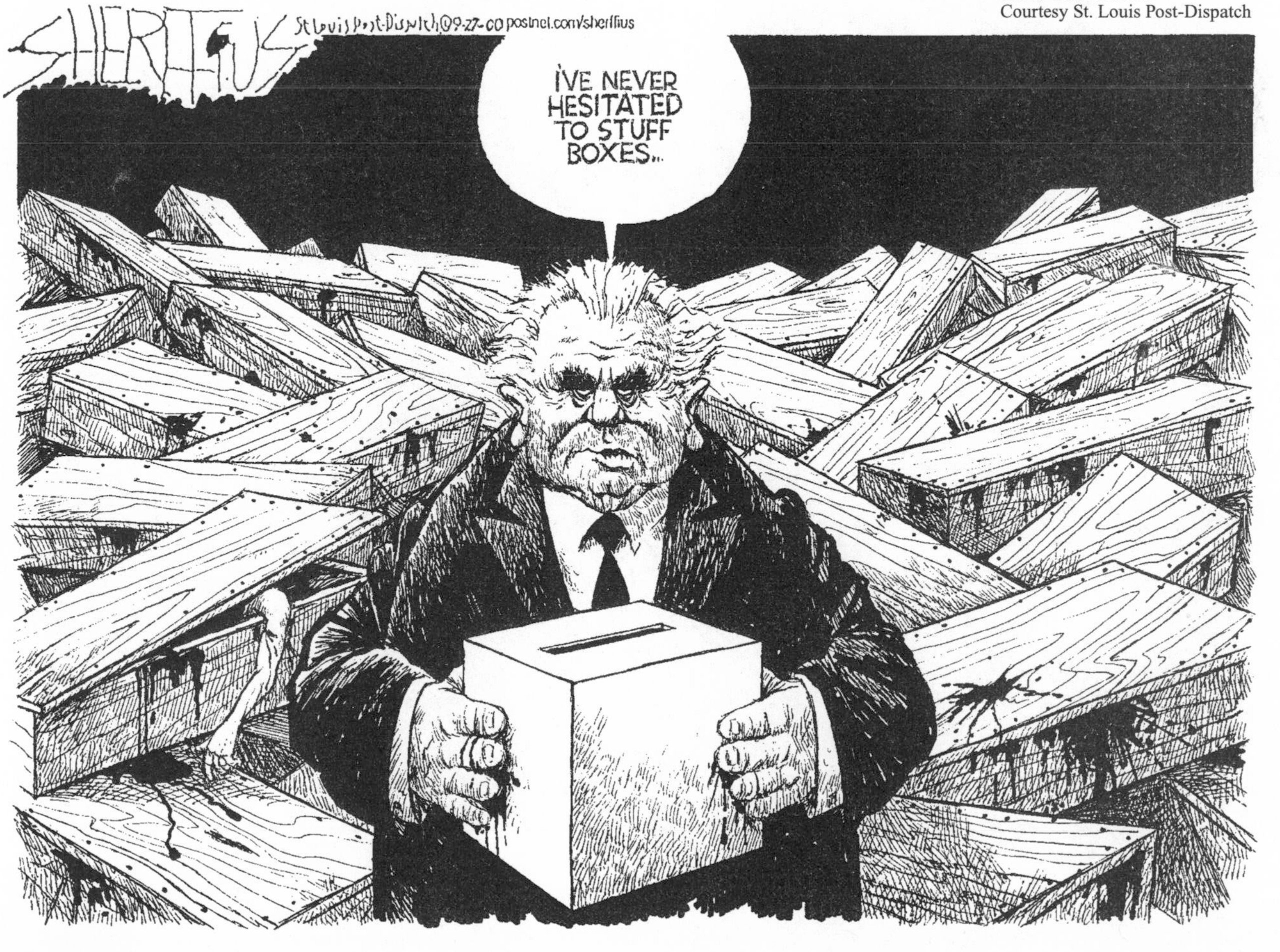
SHERFFIUS
St. Louis Post-Dispatch 9-27-00 postnet.com/sherffius
I'VE NEVER HESITATED TO STUFF BOXES...

ED STEIN
Courtesy Rocky Mountain News

ED GAMBLE
Courtesy Florida Times-Union

EDGAR SOLLER
Courtesy California Examiner

NEIL GRAHAME
Courtesy Spencer Newspapers

DENNIS DRAUGHON
Courtesy Scranton Times

SANDY CAMPBELL
Courtesy The Tennessean

LARRY WRIGHT
Courtesy Detroit News

JAMES CASCIARI
Courtesy Vero Beach Press Journal

JOEL PETT
Courtesy Lexington Herald-Leader

WAYNE STAYSKAL
Courtesy Tampa Tribune

# Berry's World

www.comics.com

© 2000 by NEA, Inc.

JIM BERRY
Courtesy NEA

LAZARO FRESQUET
Courtesy El Nuevo Herald (Miami)

KEVIN KALLAUGHER
Courtesy Baltimore Sun

RICHARD CROWSON
Courtesy Wichita Eagle

GUY BADEAUX
Courtesy LeDroit (Ottawa)

BRUCE BEATTIE
Courtesy Daytona Beach News-Journal

"OK . . . We've got the Russian economy back on its feet. Now what?!"

WORSHIPING THEIR GOD...

THE MIDEAST PEACE PROCESS IS STILL ON TRACK.

©2000 CHICAGO TRIBUNE

"YES ELIAN, SOMEDAY ALL THIS WILL BE YOURS..."

WE'RE PLEASED TO HAVE LITTLE ELIAN BACK IN HIS HOMELAND WHERE HE'S FREE TO GROW INTO THE SPECIAL INDIVIDUAL WE'RE SURE HE'LL BECOME.

PUTIN'S SUB STANCE

KURSK TRAGEDY

SUBSTANCE ON THE ROCKS?

DANIEL AGUILA
Courtesy Filipino Reporter

JON RICHARDS
Courtesy Santa Fe Reporter

WE JUST WANT WHAT'S BEST FOR THE BOY!

THE COMPASSION OF POLITICIANS

NICK ANDERSON
Courtesy Louisville Courier-Journal

THANKS, NOW GET LOST...

RULE OF LAW

STACY CURTIS
Courtesy MSNBC & The Times (Ind.)

## ELIAN LEARNS TO SPELL

BRUMSIC BRANDON
Courtesy Florida Today

WAYNE STAYSKAL
Courtesy Tampa Tribune

KEVIN KALLAUGHER
Courtesy Baltimore Sun

# The Economy

The U.S. economy continued to grow during the year, but households and corporations were accumulating mountains of debt from borrowing. The U.S. trade deficit was expected to hit a record $411 billion for the year.

Microsoft's battle with the government continued. A federal judge found that the company had engaged in unfair business practices. The finding caused a drastic drop in Microsoft stock and in technology stocks in general.

Short supplies led to a sharp increase in gasoline prices during the year. By summer, prices at the pump had climbed to $1.60 per gallon. Firestone recalled millions of potentially faulty tires after more than 100 deaths were blamed on tire separation, many of them on Ford Explorer sport utility vehicles. The problem threatened Ford's long-standing relationship with Firestone and could have long-term effects on both companies.

The Southeast suffered its second consecutive year of a drought that threatened to cost farmers millions of dollars in crop losses. The stock market was on a roller coaster ride much of the year, but appeared to return to some degree of normalcy by December. Many analysts saw the possibility of a recession looming on the horizon.

JACK HIGGINS
Courtesy Chicago Sun-Times

LARRY WRIGHT
Courtesy Detroit News

LARRY LEWIS
Courtesy Jackson Citizen Patriot (Mich.)

JIM BORGMAN
Courtesy Cincinnati Enquirer

VIC HARVILLE
Courtesy Donrey News (Ark.)

EUGENE PAYNE
Courtesy Charlotte Observer

DOUG MACGREGOR
Courtesy News Press at Fort Myers

CHAN LOWE
Courtesy Fort Lauderdale News/Sun Sentinel

EUGENE PAYNE
Courtesy Charlotte Observer

JERRY HOLBERT
Courtesy Boston Herald

FRED CURATOLO
Courtesy Edmonton Sun

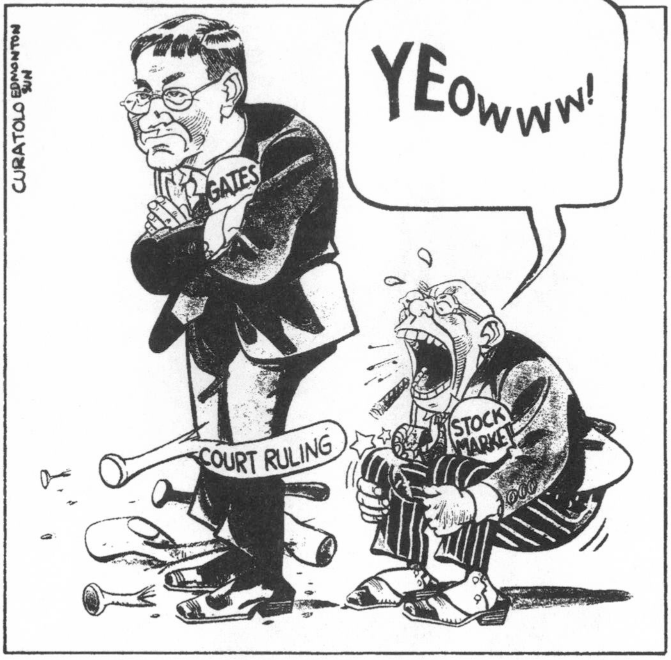
CURATOLO EDMONTON SUN
YEOWWW!
GATES
COURT RULING
STOCK MARKET

STEVE BREEN
Courtesy Asbury Park Press

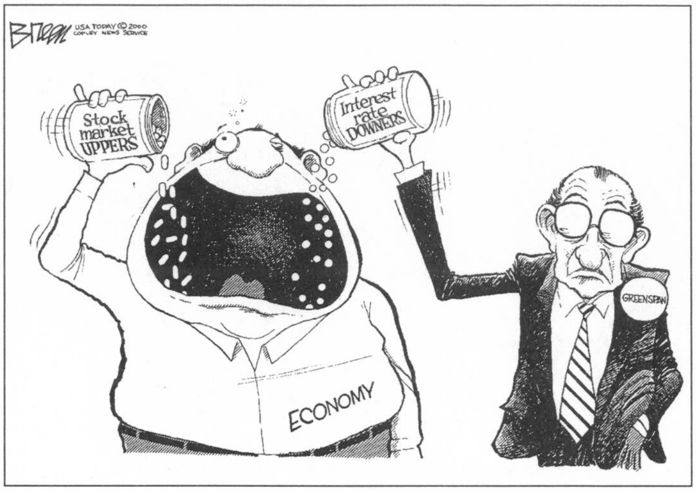
BREEN
Stock market UPPERS
Interest rate DOWNERS
ECONOMY
GREENSPAN

WALT HANDELSMAN
Courtesy New Orleans Times-Picayune

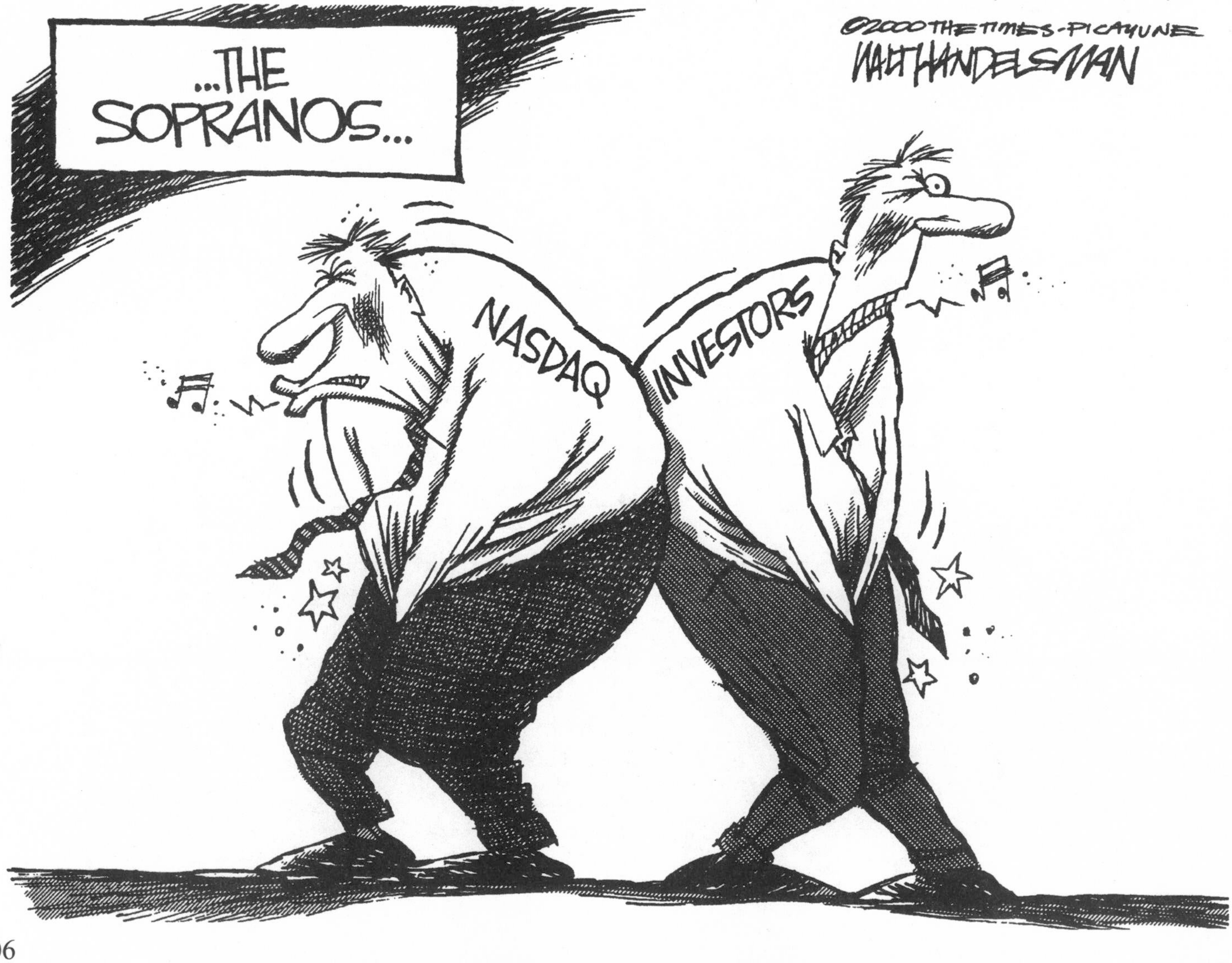
©2000 THE TIMES-PICAYUNE
WALT HANDELSMAN
...THE SOPRANOS...
NASDAQ
INVESTORS

DENNIS DRAUGHON
Courtesy Scranton Times

ROB HARRIMAN
Courtesy Polk County Itemizer Observer

PAUL CONRAD
Courtesy Los Angeles Times

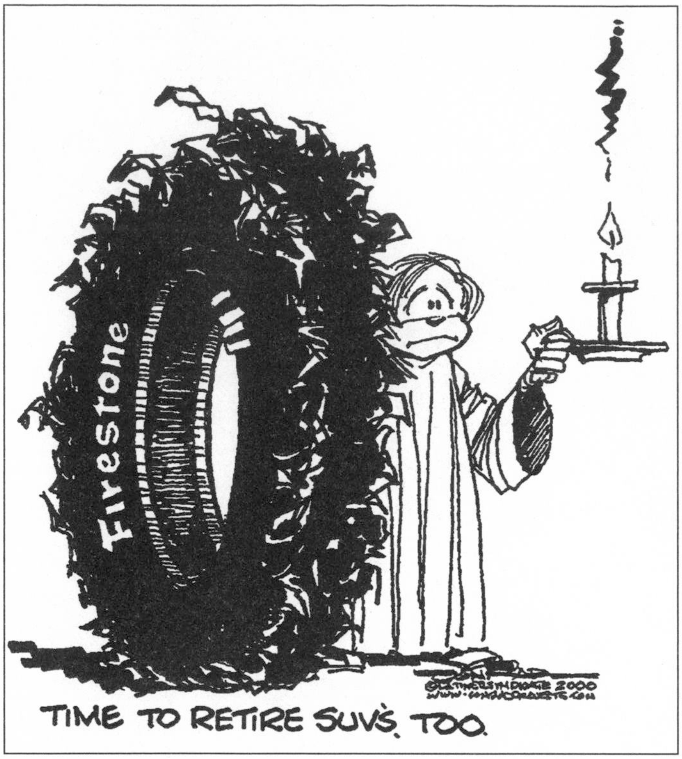

Firestone
©LA TIMES SYNDICATE 2000
TIME TO RETIRE SUVS, TOO.


JOE HOFFECKER
Courtesy Cincinnati Business Courier

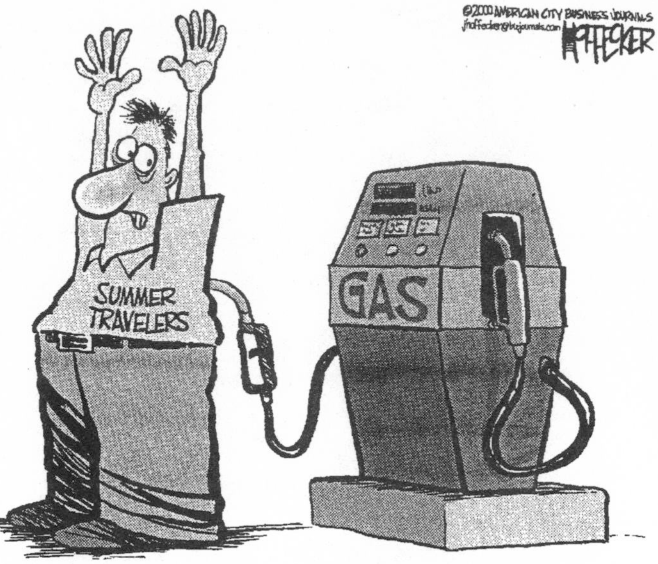

©2000 AMERICAN CITY BUSINESS JOURNALS
jhoffecker@bizjournals.com
HOFFECKER
SUMMER TRAVELERS
GAS


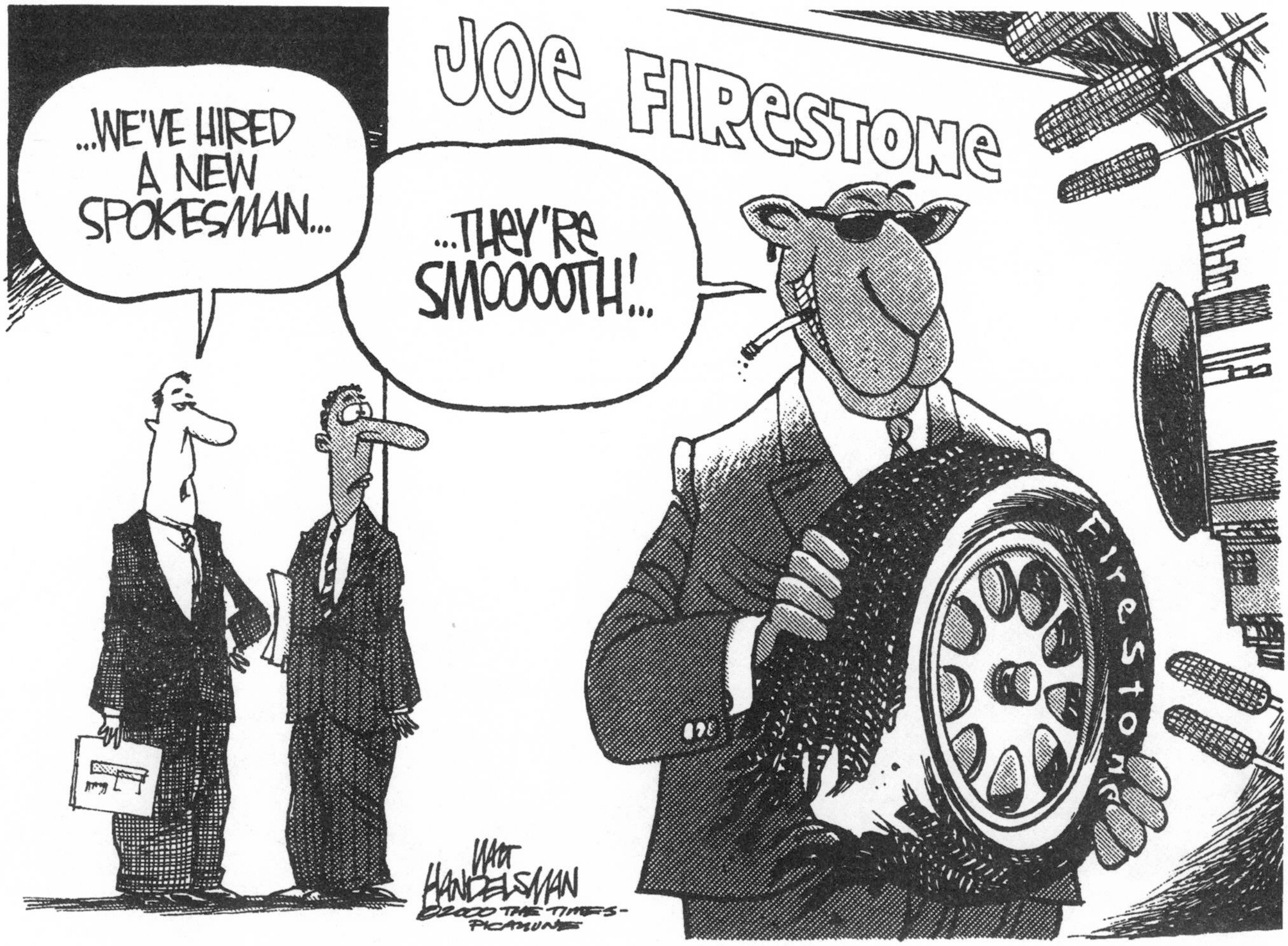

JOE FIRESTONE
...WE'VE HIRED A NEW SPOKESMAN...
...THEY'RE SMOOOOTH!...
Firestone
WALT HANDELSMAN
©2000 THE TIMES-PICAYUNE


WALT HANDELSMAN
Courtesy New Orleans Times-Picayune

JEFF MACNELLY
Courtesy Chicago Tribune

ROBERT ARIAIL
Courtesy The State (S.C.)

LARRY WRIGHT
Courtesy Detroit News

JOSEPH F. O'MAHONEY
Courtesy The Enterprise (Mass.)

KIRK ANDERSON
Courtesy St. Paul Pioneer Press

INVISIBLE HANDS OF THE MARKET

STEPHEN TEMPLETON
Courtesy Fayetteville Observer-Times (N.C.)

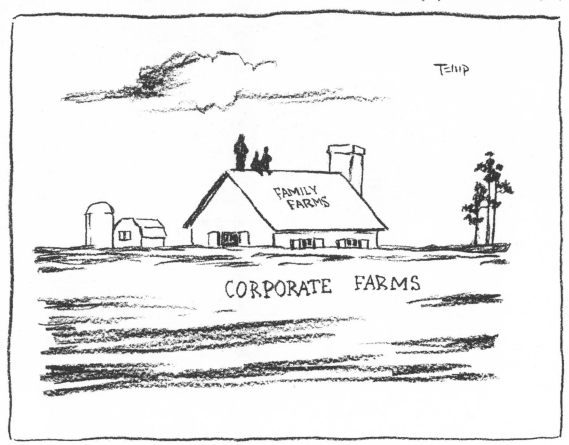

MICKEY SIPORIN
Courtesy Los Angeles Times

SANDY CAMPBELL
Courtesy The Tennessean

BOB ENGLEHART
Courtesy Hartford Courant

BOB RICH
Courtesy Connecticut Post

DAVE GRANLUND
Courtesy Metrowest Daily News (Mass.)

J. R. ROSE
Courtesy Byrd Newspapers

JAMES CASCIARI
Courtesy Vero Beach Press Journal

JERRY BARNETT
Courtesy Indianapolis News

ELENA STEIR
Courtesy The Valley News (Conn.)

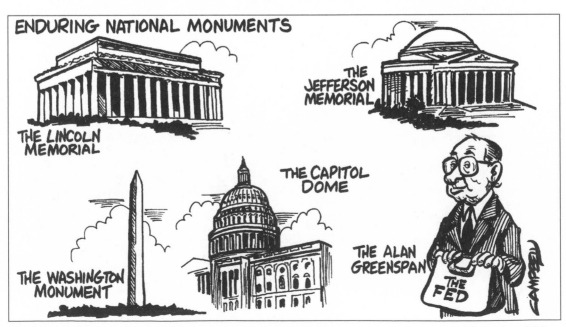

SANDY CAMPBELL
Courtesy The Tennessean

114

DON LANDGREN, JR.
Courtesy The Landmark (Mass.)

JAMES CASCIARI
Courtesy Vero Beach Press Journal

FRANK CAMMUSO
Courtesy Syracuse Herald-Journal

JOHN MARSHALL
Courtesy Binghamton Press and Sun-Bulletin

# Politics

One of the most highly respected and influential lawmakers in Washington, Democratic Sen. Daniel Patrick Moynihan of New York, announced his retirement, setting off a mad scramble to choose his successor. The tenacious former prosecutor and mayor of New York Rudy Giuliani announced his candidacy, as did President Clinton's wife, Hillary. Giuliani, however, withdrew because of health problems, and a virtually unknown congressman, Rick Lazio, replaced him. Despite accusations of being a New Yorker-come-lately, Hillary won in a landslide.

Citing "serious misconduct," an Arkansas disciplinary panel recommended that President Clinton be disbarred for giving misleading testimony—some called it lying—about his relationship with Monica Lewinsky. It was an unprecedented rebuke for a sitting president. Whitewater investigators finally announced that neither the president nor his wife would be charged in that fiasco.

Congress talked a lot about campaign finance abuses, but took no real action to fix the problem. Atty. Gen. Janet Reno once again refused to name an independent counsel to investigate wrongdoing in the Clinton—Gore administration when asked to look into Gore's fundraising role in the 1996 campaign.

RICK MCKEE
Courtesy Augusta Chronicle

"I HAVEN'T HEARD A DEMOCRAT MENTION 'GOD' THIS MANY TIMES SINCE HILLARY HIT HER THUMB WITH A HAMMER!...."

EVOLUTION OF THE G.O.P.SAURUS...

REAGAN PERIOD... GINGRICH PERIOD... W. BUSH PERIOD...

BEN SARGENT
Courtesy Austin American-Statesman

THE HARROWING VOYAGE TO AMERICA

THE HARROWING VOYAGE HOME

ED STEIN
Courtesy Rocky Mountain News

MICHAEL OSBUN
Courtesy Sumter County Times (Fla.)

CHESTER COMMODORE
Courtesy Chicago Defender

CHIP BECK
Courtesy The Real Washington

LINDA BOILEAU
Courtesy Frankfort State Journal

JIMMY MARGULIES
Courtesy Hackensack Record

DOUG REGALIA
Courtesy Contra Costa Times (Calif.)

JON RICHARDS
Courtesy Santa Fe Reporter

PAM WINTERS
Courtesy San Diego Union-Tribune

MICHAEL RAMIREZ
Courtesy Los Angeles Times

THE DEATH OF CIVILITY

# Society

Y2K, the much-ballyhooed computer disaster-to-be, came and went with barely a glitch. Billions of dollars were spent by U.S. corporations to head off potential Y2K problems, while countries such as Italy and Pakistan spent virtually nothing and still experienced few difficulties.

In a historic move, Pope John Paul II in March visited the Middle East, where he asked for forgiveness for Catholics for unspecified sins. Some critics were disappointed that he did not specifically mention the church's lack of protest during the Holocaust, when 6 million Jews perished under Nazi rule.

The U.S. Supreme Court in June upheld the Boy Scouts' ban on gay Scout leaders. This policy has been denounced as discriminatory by school boards and corporations, some of which have ended or reduced support for the youth organization.

Reality entertainment blossomed as a popular fad, spurred by the CBS show "Survivor," where 16 people were stranded on a desert island and eliminated one by one through "tribal" voting. The last person on the island won a million dollars.

Rage in America reached its limits in Alabama when a woman driver shot and killed another in a fit of anger over a traffic altercation. Vermont became the first state to give gay and lesbian couples virtually all the rights and benefits of marriage.

DAVID REDDICK
Courtesy Anderson Herald Bulletin (Ind.)

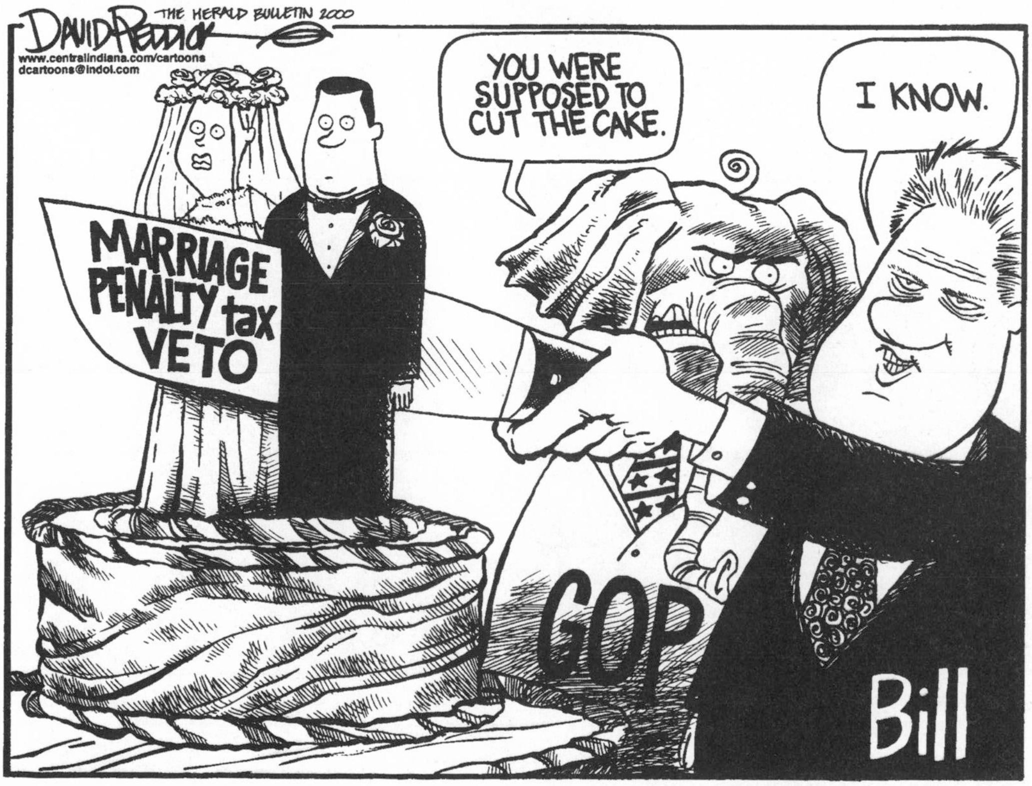
DAVID REDDICK
THE HERALD BULLETIN 2000
www.centralindiana.com/cartoons
dcartoons@indol.com
YOU WERE SUPPOSED TO CUT THE CAKE.
I KNOW.
MARRIAGE PENALTY tax VETO
GOP
Bill

CINDY PROCIOUS
Courtesy Huntsville Times

JOHN TREVER
Courtesy Albuquerque Journal

BARBARA BRANDON-CROFT
Courtesy Universal Press Syndicate

MICHAEL THOMPSON
Courtesy Detroit Free Press

ANN CLEAVES
Courtesy Palisadian Post (Calif.)

125

THE MORE THINGS CHANGE THE MORE THEY REMAIN THE SAME

JIM LANGE
Courtesy The Daily Oklahoman

RUSSELL HODIN
Courtesy The New Times (Calif.)

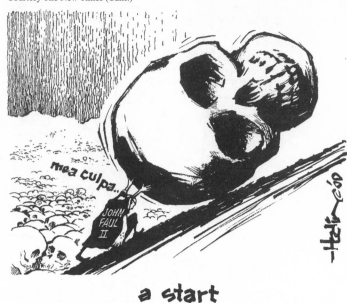

mea culpa..

JOHN PAUL II

a start

MIKE PETERS
Courtesy Dayton Daily News

©2000 DAYTON DAILY NEWS TRIBUNE MEDIA SERVICES

YOU'RE NOT GAY ARE YOU?

WAYNE STAYSKAL
Courtesy Tampa Tribune

JOHN MARSHALL
Courtesy Binghamton Press and Sun-Bulletin

JOE LONG
Courtesy Observer-Dispatch (N.Y.)

PATRICK ALAN RICE
Courtesy Jupiter Courier

CHAN LOWE
Courtesy Fort Lauderdale News/Sun Sentinel

JOHN SPENCER
Courtesy Philadelphia Business Journal

NICK ANDERSON
Courtesy Louisville Courier-Journal

JOE HELLER
Courtesy Green Bay Press-Gazette

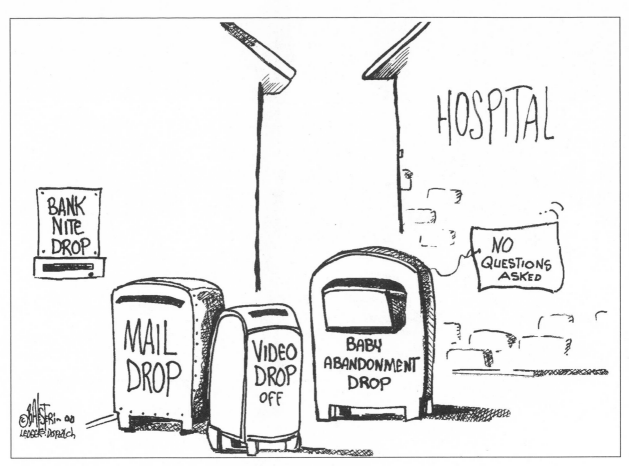

ANNETTE BALESTERI
Courtesy Antioch Ledger Dispatch (Calif.)

JAMES MCCLOSKEY
Courtesy Staunton Daily News Leader (Va.)

131

BRUCE BEATTIE
Courtesy Daytona Beach News-Journal

"Now, now . . . we have to get used to wearing this stuff in case
the inheritance tax gets repealed."

JOE MAJESKI
Courtesy Times-Leader (Pa.)

VERMONT GOTHIC

STEVE BREEN
Courtesy Asbury Park Press

ANNETTE BALESTERI
Courtesy Antioch Ledger Dispatch (Calif.)

DAVE SATTLER
Courtesy Lafayette Journal Courier (Ind.)

ED FISCHER
Courtesy Rochester Post-Bulletin

JOHN WEISS
Courtesy San Cruz Sentinel (Calif.)

# Education

Students at Columbine High School in Colorado had cause to grieve anew during the year when two teenage sweethearts were shot in a Littleton sandwich shop. The shooting came less than a year after two students went on a shooting spree at Columbine High. A month later, another shocking killing took place in a Michigan elementary school. A six-year-old boy shot and killed a six-year-old girl following an argument. Children carrying guns to school remained a startling fact of life.

A Florida circuit judge overturned the nation's first statewide school voucher program. Congress argued, as did teachers and parents across the land, over various voucher programs that would use public dollars to send children to private schools.

Lawmakers in many states worked to have the Ten Commandments displayed in schools. Supporters of the idea claim it would help to curb school violence. The action remains highly controversial, however, and opponents have vowed to challenge any proposed legislation supporting it.

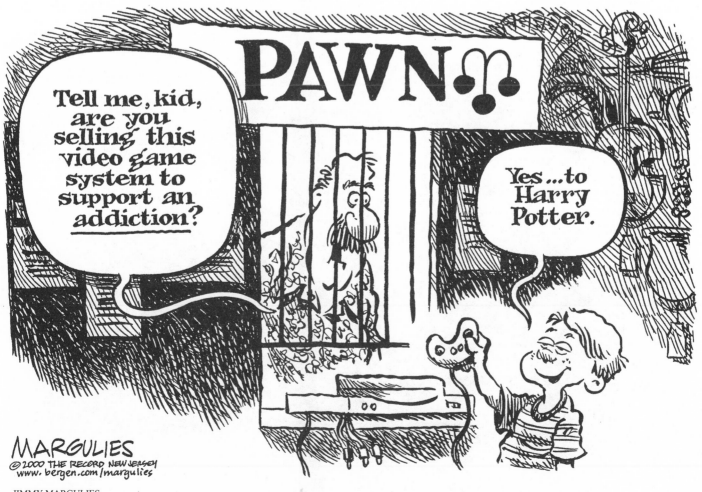

MARGULIES
© 2000 THE RECORD NEW JERSEY
www.bergen.com/margulies

JIMMY MARGULIES
Courtesy Hackensack Record

135

HANK MCCLURE
Courtesy Lawton Constitution

JOHN KNUDSEN
Courtesy St. Louis Review

JOHN WEISS
Courtesy San Cruz Sentinel (Calif.)

136

STEVE BREEN
Courtesy Asbury Park Press

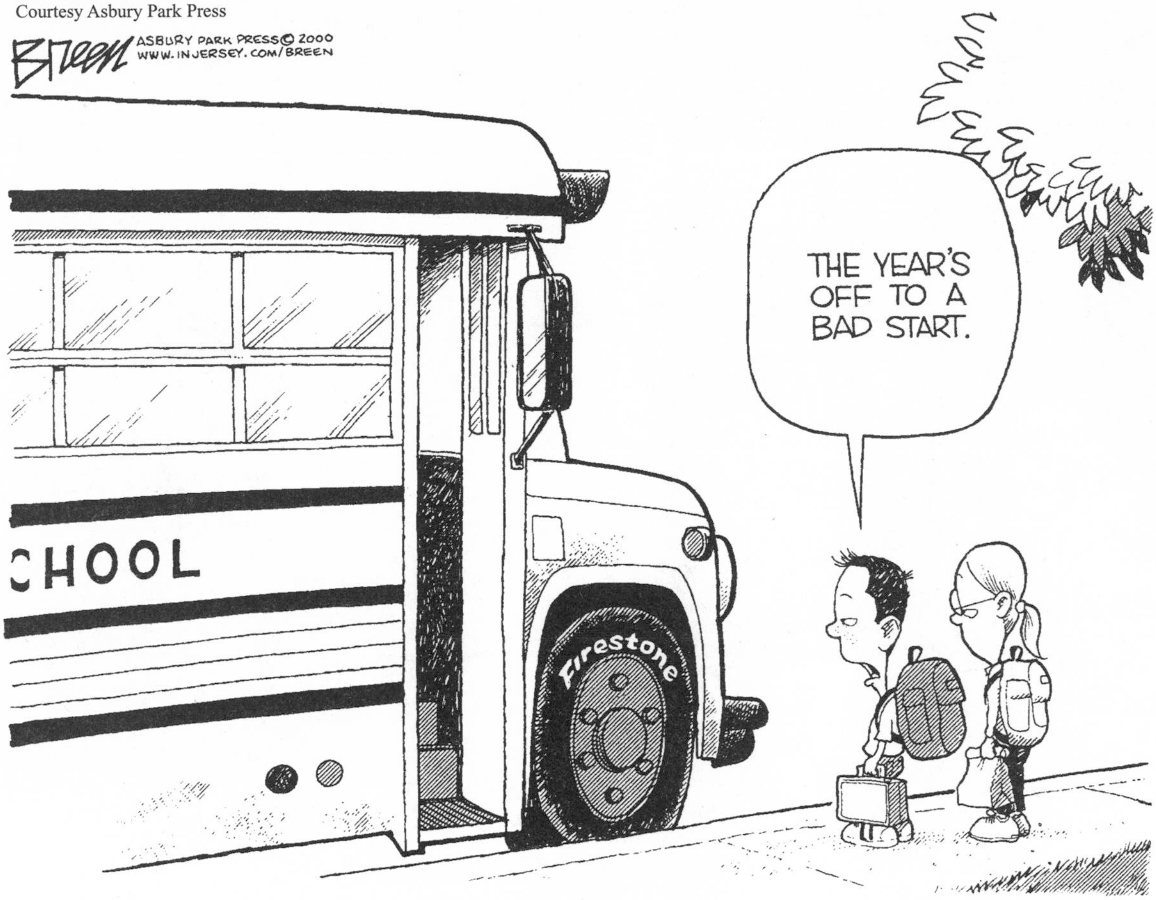
BREEN
ASBURY PARK PRESS© 2000
WWW.INJERSEY.COM/BREEN
THE YEAR'S OFF TO A BAD START.
CHOOL
Firestone

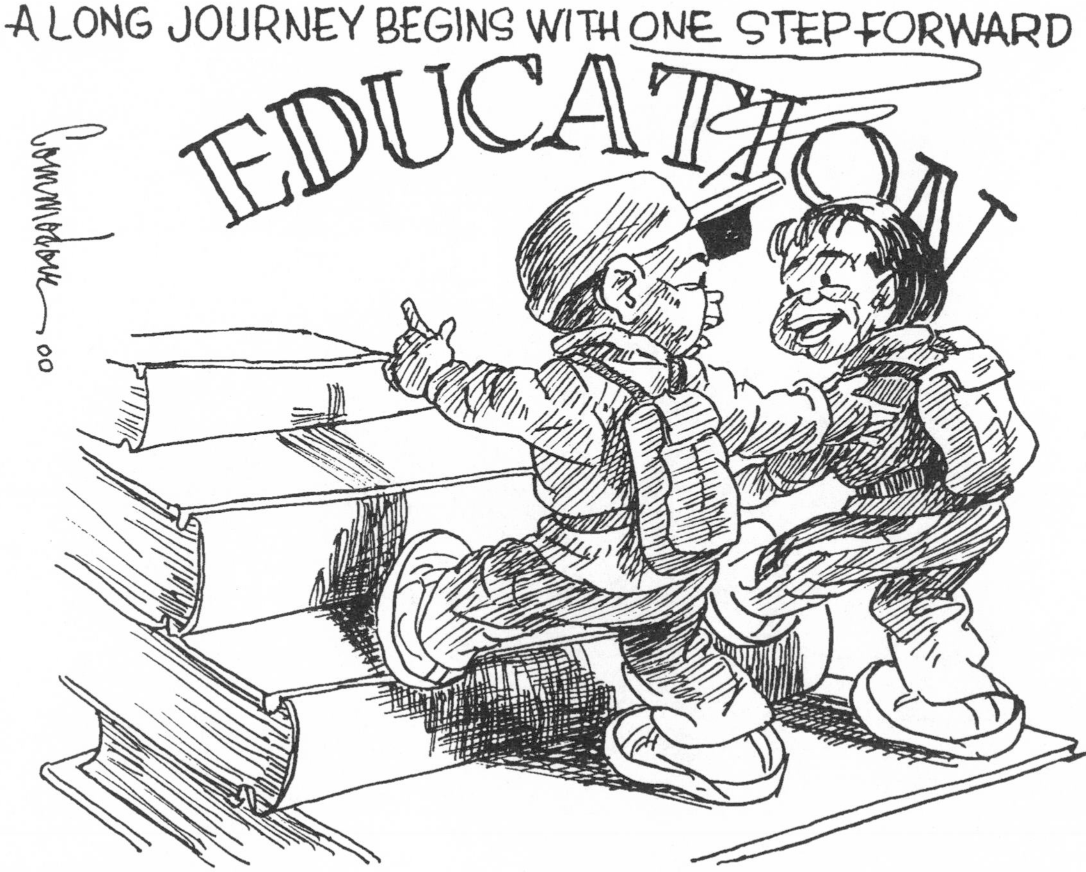
A LONG JOURNEY BEGINS WITH ONE STEP FORWARD
EDUCATION
Commodore 00

CHESTER COMMODORE
Courtesy Chicago Defender

MARSHALL RAMSEY
Courtesy Jackson Clarion-Ledger (Miss.)

CHARLES DANIEL
Courtesy Knoxville News-Sentinel

YOU CAN'T BE TOO CAREFUL!

JIM LANGE
Courtesy The Daily Oklahoman

JOHN SHERFFIUS
Courtesy St. Louis Post-Dispatch

139

STEVE MCBRIDE
Courtesy Independence Daily Reporter (Kan.)

BRIAN DUFFY
Courtesy Des Moines Register

# Health

Scientists announced early in 2000 the completion of a momentous task—the mapping of the entire human genetic code. The information, which took many years to assemble, could lead to cures for cancer, Alzheimer's disease, and diabetes.

In Miami, jurors hit Big Tobacco with the largest punitive damages verdict in history, a whopping $145 billion. The industry is paying a total of $246 billion to settle health claims in the 50 states. Philip Morris vowed to pursue every possible avenue of appeal. Tobacco consumption is down just 1 to 2 percent from last year, and people are continuing to smoke. A recent report estimates that smoking is increasing among 18- to 24-year olds.

The cost of prescription drugs continued to rise, imposing a burden on the elderly, who tend to use more medicine. Congress has been looking into the problem but so far has failed to come up with relief for buyers. During the presidential campaign, both major candidates pledged to find solutions to the prescription drug problem.

In June, the U.S. Supreme Court ruled that patients cannot sue their health plans in federal court for rewarding doctors who hold down costs.

DAVID HITCH
Courtesy Worcester Telegram and Gazette

ED HALL
Courtesy Baker County Press (Fla.)

STEVE NEASE
Courtesy Niagara Falls Review

RICK MCKEE
Courtesy Augusta Chronicle

GLENN MCCOY
Courtesy Belleville News-Democrat (Ill.)

BRUMSIC BRANDON
Courtesy Florida Today

JERRY SELTZER
Courtesy Tallahassee Democrat

BOB RICH
Courtesy Connecticut Post

GARY VARVEL
Courtesy Indianapolis Star

HUMAN GENETICS RESEARCH

JIM DYKE
JEFFERSON CITY
NEWS TRIBUNE
©2000

JIM DYKE
Courtesy Jefferson City News Tribune

TOM GIBB
The Tribune-Democrat

THE TRIBUNE-DEMOCRAT
GIBB
©2000

TOBACCO COMPANIES SAY THAT THE $145 BILLION VERDICT AGAINST THEM COULD RUIN THEM.

STAND BY...WE'RE GONNA SMOKE ONE.

BIG OL' TOBACCO

IN AMERICA, THAT'S CALLED EXECUTING A KILLER

145

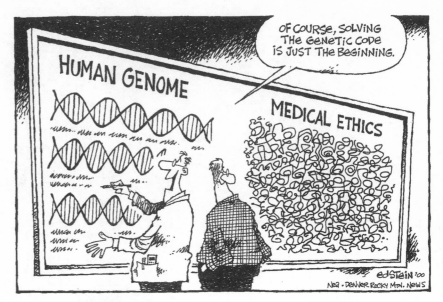

ED STEIN
Courtesy Rocky Mountain News

SCOTT BATEMAN
Courtesy North American Syndicate

S. C. RAWLS
Courtesy NEA

146

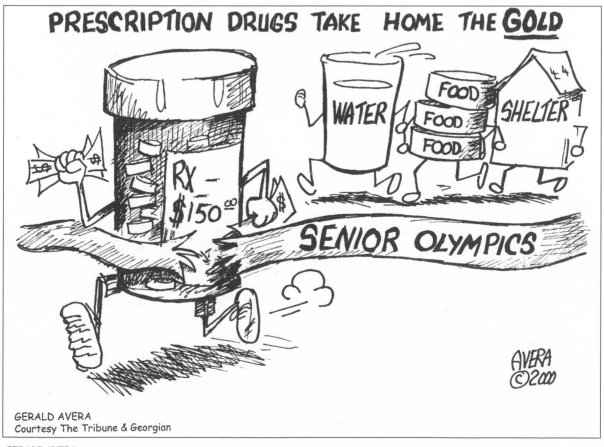

GERALD AVERA
Courtesy The Tribune & Georgian

GERALD AVERA
Courtesy Tribune & Georgian (Ga.)

JEFF PARKER
Courtesy Florida Today

DREW SHENEMAN
Courtesy Newark Star-Ledger

# Crime

Worried about the possibility of the state taking an innocent life, Gov. George Ryan made Illinois the first to declare a halt to executions. Thirteen prisoners had been exonerated and released from death row since 1977, while 12 had been executed. Ryan appointed a commission to study the problem during the moratorium. Similarly questionable cases were uncovered in 37 other death-penalty states, where 85 death-row inmates have been exonerated since 1973. Several states announced they were studying the matter.

Police problems have long plagued big cities. During the year, a cameraman on a television news helicopter in Philadelphia captured on film the beating of a suspect by several cops. The incident was publicized throughout the country. Tales of police abuse kept cropping up in other cities, but police maintain that suspects simply have become more militant and more likely to resist arrest.

The New York shooting of West African immigrant Amadov Diallo gained national attention. Four policemen shot the unarmed man they believed to be a serial rapist 41 times.

BEN SARGENT
Courtesy Austin American-Statesman

JOEL PETT
Courtesy Lexington Herald-Leader

JONATHAN TODD
Courtesy Herald Journal and Post-Standard (N.Y.)

BARBARA BRANDON-CROFT
Courtesy Universal Press Syndicate

PAUL CONRAD
Courtesy Los Angeles Times

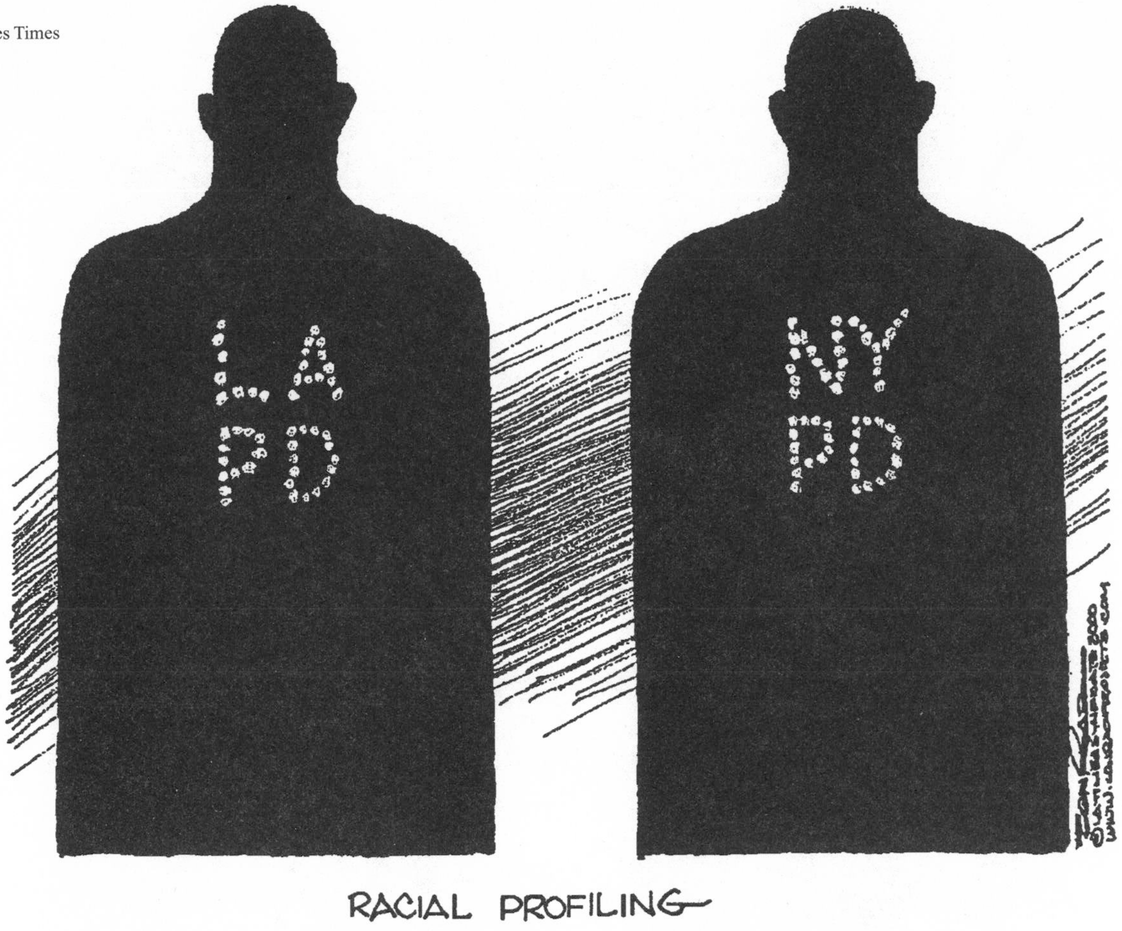
LA PD
NY PD
RACIAL PROFILING—

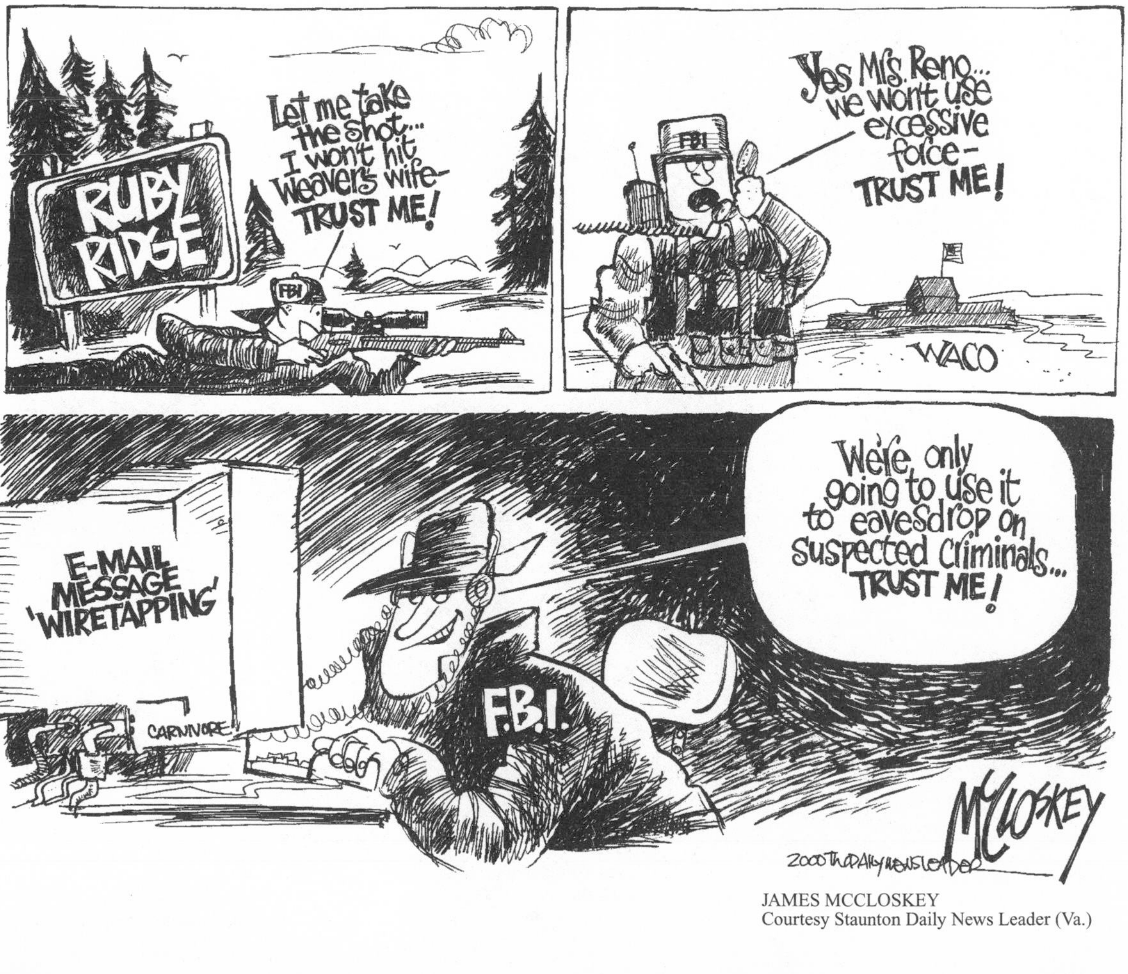
RUBY RIDGE
Let me take the shot... I won't hit Weaver's wife– TRUST ME!
FBI
Yes Mrs. Reno... we won't use excessive force– TRUST ME!
FBI
WACO
E-MAIL MESSAGE 'WIRETAPPING'
CARNIVORE
We're only going to use it to eavesdrop on suspected criminals... TRUST ME!
F.B.I.
MCCLOSKEY

JAMES MCCLOSKEY
Courtesy Staunton Daily News Leader (Va.)

NEWS ITEM: 68% OF DEATH PENALTIES OVERTURNED

VIC HARVILLE
Courtesy Donrey News (Ark.)

BRUCE QUAST
Courtesy Rockford Register-Star

ARTHUR HENRIKSON
Courtesy Des Plaines Daily Herald

CLAY BENNETT
Courtesy Christian Science Monitor

JIM DYKE
Courtesy Jefferson City News Tribune

MICHAEL THOMPSON
Courtesy Detroit Free Press

154

WAYNE STAYSKAL
Courtesy Tampa Tribune

BRIAN DUFFY
Courtesy Des Moines Register

FINALLY FOUND IN THE RUBBLE

DOUG REGALIA
Courtesy Contra Costa Times (Calif.)

ALAN VITELLO
Courtesy Greeley Tribune (Col.)

WHEN A HAND THAT SHOULD HOLD A CRAYON INSTEAD HOLDS A GUN.

CLAY BENNETT
Courtesy Christian Science Monitor

# Gun Control

Actor Charlton Heston, president of the National Rifle Association, remained a perennial target of gun control activists. The torrent of criticism, however, did not deter him from sounding off in defending personal freedoms and the right to bear arms.

The shooting of a six-year-old girl by a six-year-old boy at an elementary school in Michigan set off demands for more stringent controls on guns everywhere. President Clinton met with congressional leaders to push for more meaningful legislation.

Mothers concerned about gun violence marched on Washington, D.C. in what was billed as the Million Mom March, demanding stricter gun control laws, including a requirement for trigger locks. As with so many other issues facing America, citizens remain deeply divided over how best to control lethal weapons.

STEVE LINDSTROM
Courtesy Duluth News-Tribune

BILL VALLADARES
Courtesy Montclair Times (N.J.)

JAKE FULLER
Courtesy Gainesville Sun

DENNIS DRAUGHON
Courtesy Scranton Times

158

JEFF MACNELLY
Courtesy Chicago Tribune

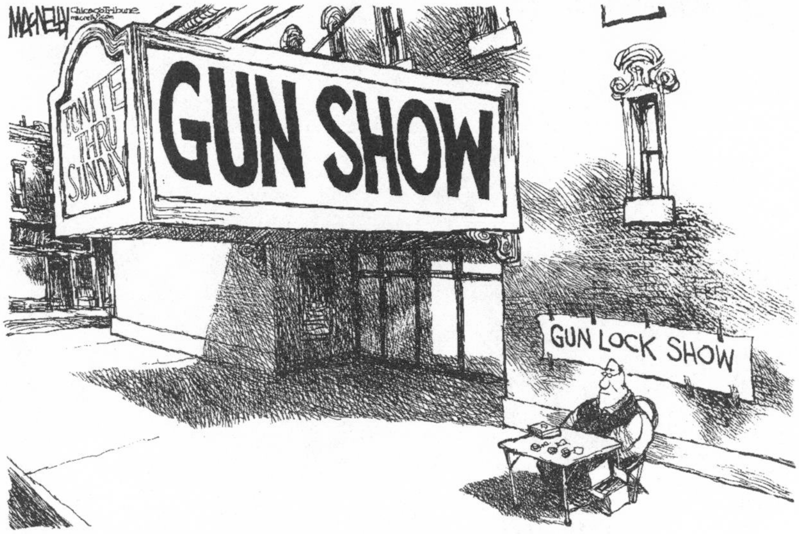
MACNELLY
TONITE THRU SUNDAY
GUN SHOW
GUN LOCK SHOW



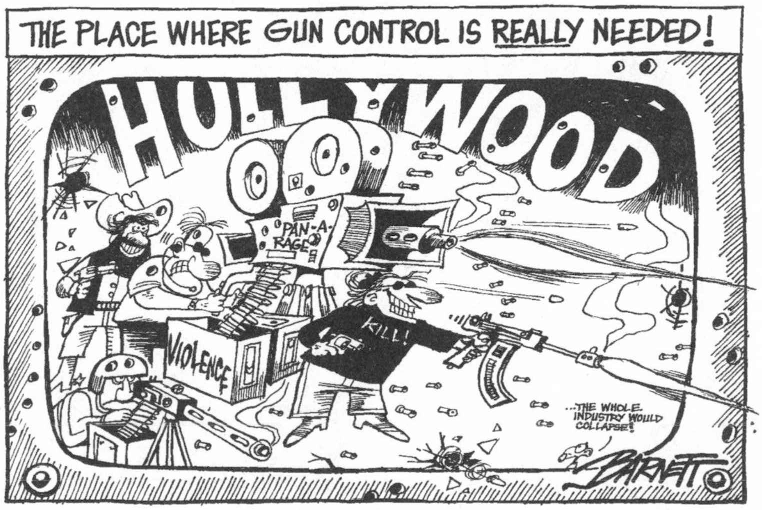
THE PLACE WHERE GUN CONTROL IS REALLY NEEDED!
HOLLYWOOD
PAN-A RAGE
KILL!
VIOLENCE
...THE WHOLE INDUSTRY WOULD COLLAPSE!
BARNETT

JERRY BARNETT
Courtesy Indianapolis News

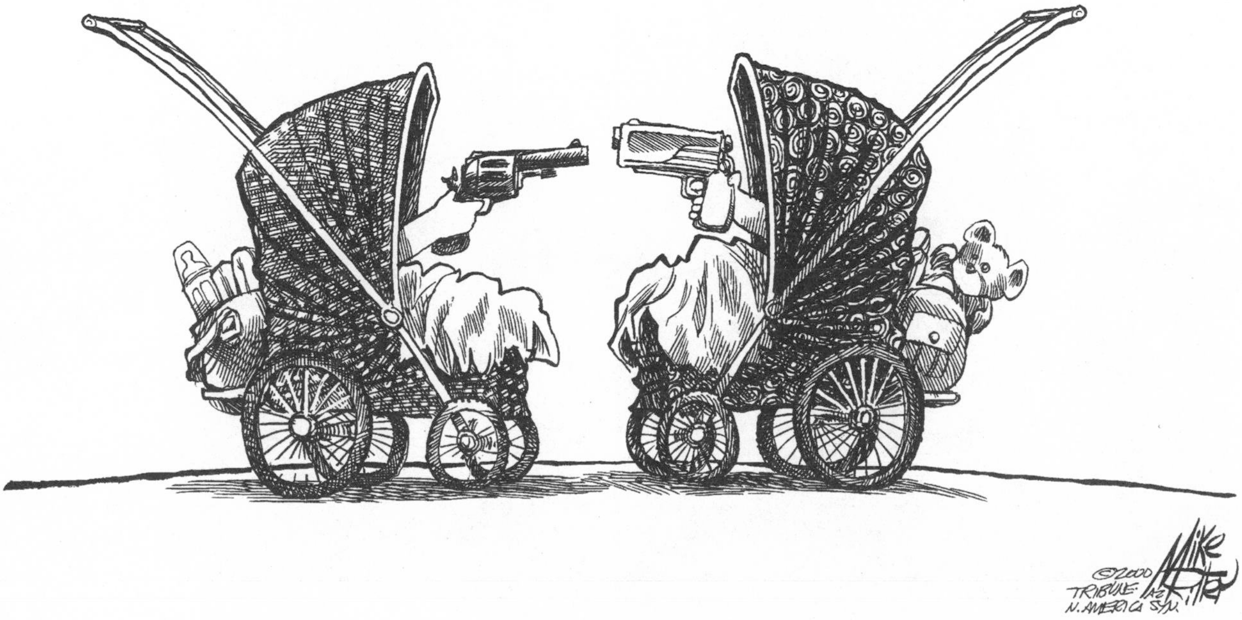
©2000 TRIBUNE MEDIA N. AMERICA SYN.
MIKE RITTER

MIKE RITTER
Courtesy Tribune Newspapers

CARLOS E. GARY
Courtesy Chicago Tribune

KEN DAVIS
Courtesy Cedartown Standard (Ga.)

# Sports

Golf superstar Tiger Woods continued to dominate the sport during the year. He entered 17 tournaments and won 9 of them, including the U.S. Open, the British Open, and the PGA Championship. His earnings for the year totaled $7.9 million, and personal endorsements generated many millions more.

Atlanta Braves pitcher John Rocker came under fire for his disparaging comments about blacks, gays, and foreigners. The Braves organization fined and suspended him for his remarks, but the sanctions were later reduced. Bobby Knight, the legendary basketball coach at Indiana University, was fired when a videotape aired in April showing him grabbing a player by the throat. Knight had guided the Hoosiers to three national championships, but the university president pointed to a "pattern of unacceptable behavior" that could no longer be ignored.

Illegal drug use tarnished the Summer Olympics in Sydney, Australia. Television ratings of the spectacle were down because the games were taking place in the middle of the night in America. Furthermore, the antics of many American athletes embarrassed officials. The U.S. men won the gold in basketball, and American wrestler Rulon Gardner ended the 13-year undefeated run of Russian super heavyweight Alexander Karelin.

The New York Yankees beat the New York Mets 4 games to 1 in the Subway World Series.

JERRY BARNETT
Courtesy Indianapolis News

STEVE BREEN
Courtesy Asbury Park Press

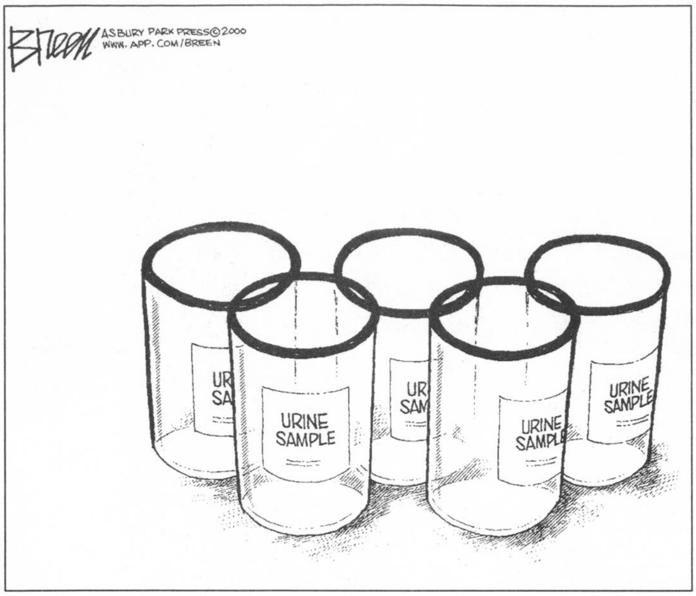
BREEN ASBURY PARK PRESS©2000
WWW.APP.COM/BREEN
URINE SAMPLE
URINE SAMPLE
URINE SAMPLE

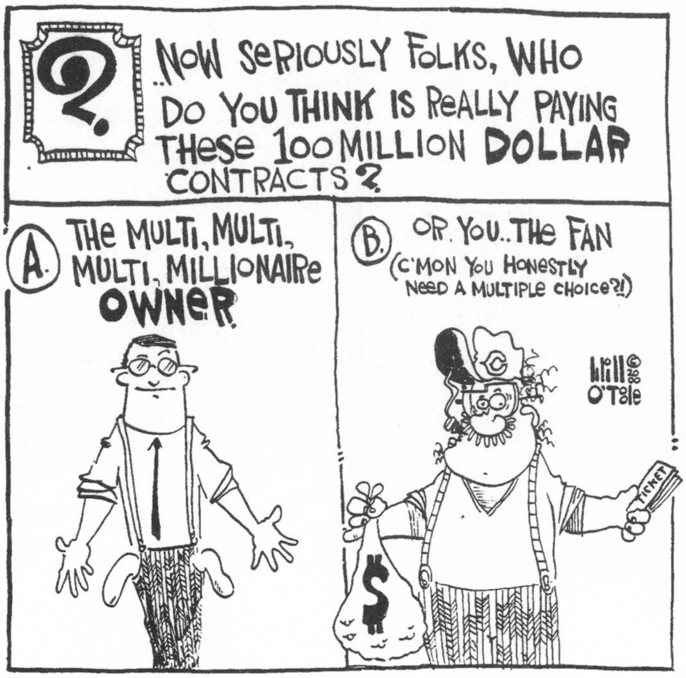
?
NOW SERIOUSLY FOLKS, WHO DO YOU THINK IS REALLY PAYING THESE 100 MILLION DOLLAR CONTRACTS?
A. THE MULTI, MULTI, MULTI, MILLIONAIRE OWNER
B. OR, YOU..THE FAN
(C'MON YOU HONESTLY NEED A MULTIPLE CHOICE?!)
$
TICKET
Will O'Toole

WILL O'TOOLE
Courtesy Home News & Tribune (N.J.)

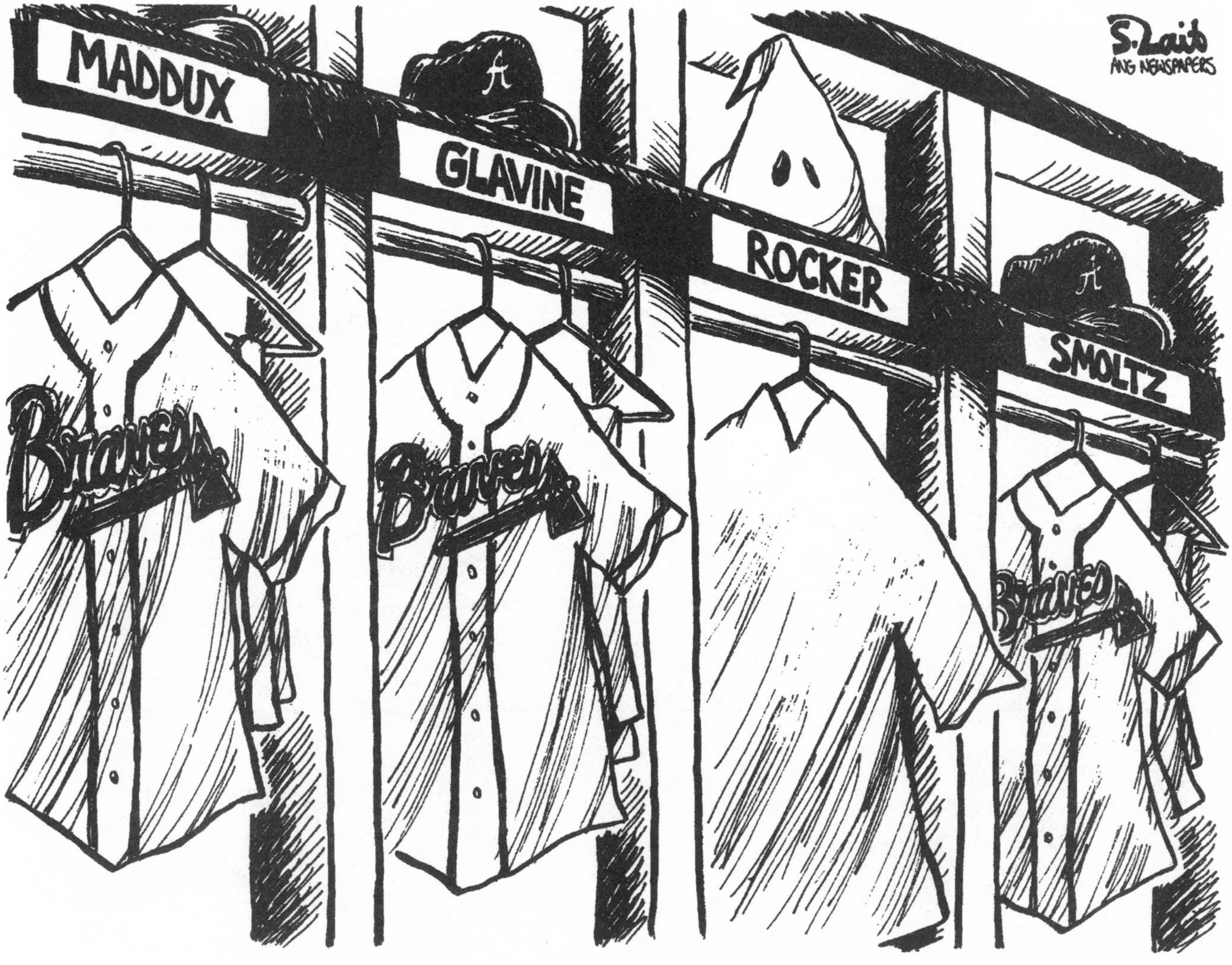
S. Lait
ANG NEWSPAPERS
MADDUX
GLAVINE
ROCKER
SMOLTZ
Braves
Braves
Braves

STEVEN LAIT
Courtesy Oakland Tribune

THE IDEAL ENDING TO the "SUBWAY SERIES"

Olympic performance-enhancing drugs...

WILL O'TOOLE
Courtesy Home News & Tribune (N.J.)

GARY VARVEL
Courtesy Indianapolis Star

BRIAN DUFFY
Courtesy Des Moines Register

164

ROB ROGERS
Courtesy Pittsburgh Post-Gazette

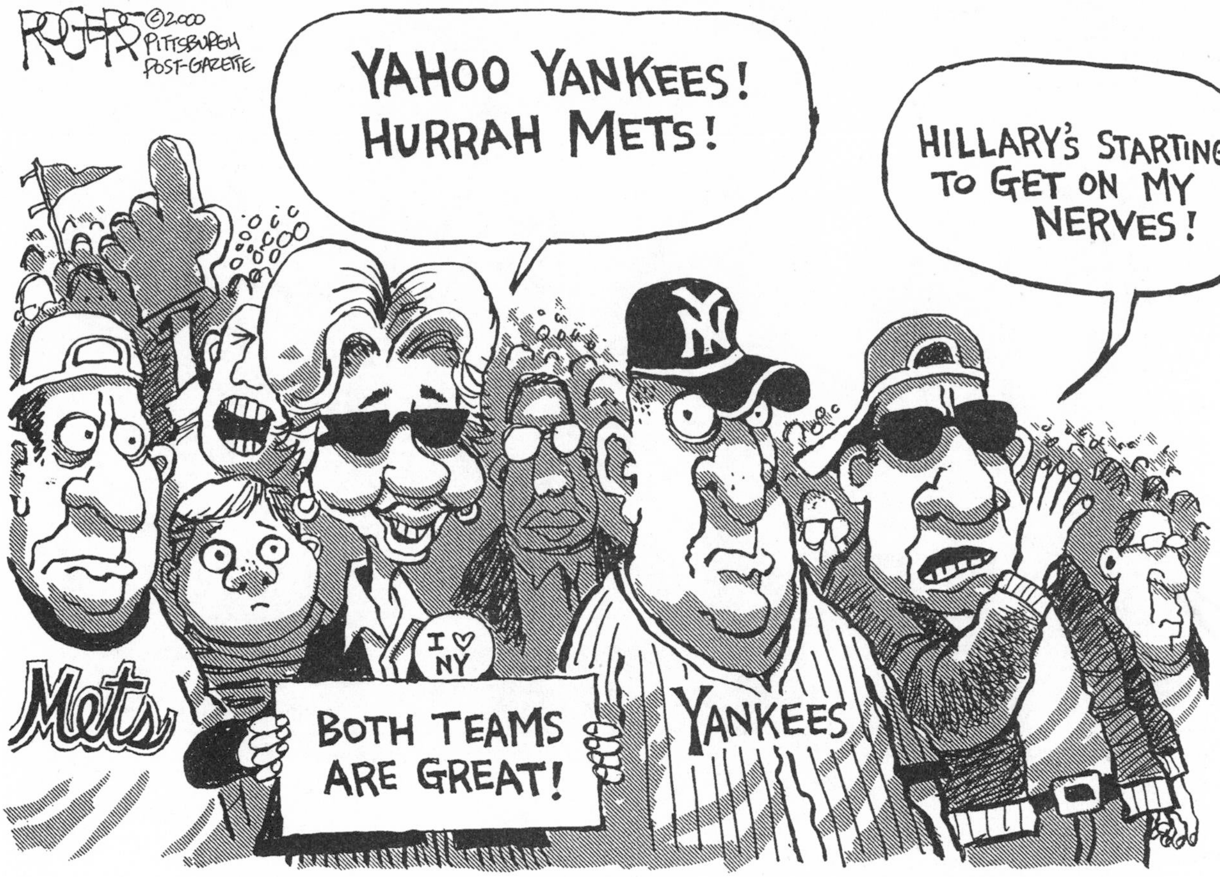
ROGERS ©2000 PITTSBURGH POST-GAZETTE
YAHOO YANKEES! HURRAH METS!
HILLARY'S STARTING TO GET ON MY NERVES!
Mets
I ♡ NY
BOTH TEAMS ARE GREAT!
YANKEES
NY

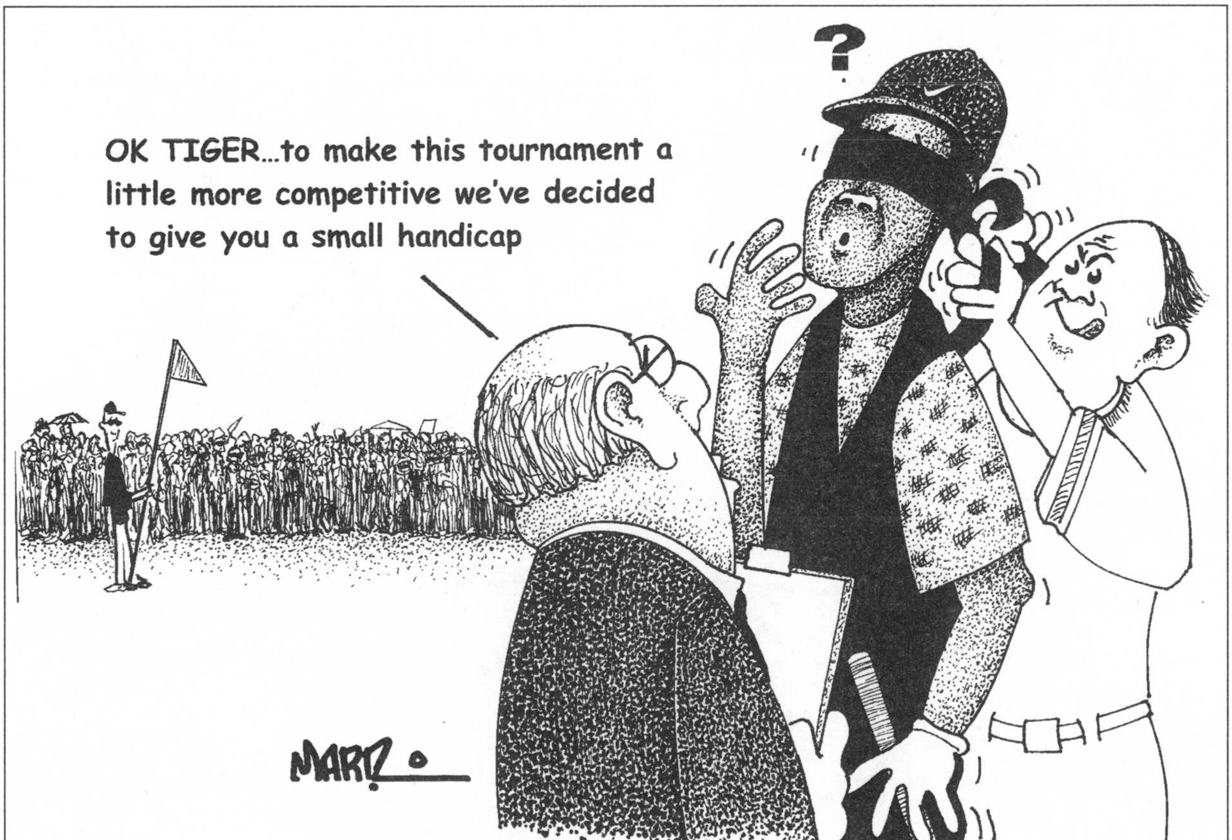
?
OK TIGER...to make this tournament a little more competitive we've decided to give you a small handicap
MARRO

DON MARQUIS
Courtesy Paradise Post (Calif.)

KERRY JOHNSON
Courtesy New Pittsburgh Courier

TOM GIBB
Courtesy The Tribune-Democrat

# Media and Movies

The media enjoyed a feeding frenzy over the case of six-year-old Elian Gonzalez, whose mother drowned in an attempt to flee to the United States from Cuba. Then, in the presidential election on November 7, television newscasts jumped the gun and announced that Al Gore had won Florida's 25 electoral votes—this while some voting places were still open in Florida, apparently deterring many Floridians from voting at all. Then the networks retracted the declaration and named George Bush the winner. Then, a few hours later, the same news organizations retracted their reports once more and acknowledged they didn't know who had won.

President Clinton and Gore continued nonstop fundraising among the Hollywood elite, assuring the entertainment crowd that they had no reason to worry about censorship. And, to no one's surprise, sex, violence, and "anything goes" themes continued to roll out of Hollywood. Television has promised to take steps to clean up its act, but little proof was forthcoming in 2000.

A student in the Philippines allegedly unleashed a virus that infected millions of computers worldwide, causing more than $10 billion in damages. For the first time, governments around the world joined in seeking assistance from the computer industry to help curb future disasters.

VIC HARVILLE
Courtesy Donrey News (Ark.)

DANIEL FENECH
Courtesy Saline Reporter (Mich.)

BILL WHITEHEAD
Courtesy Kansas City Business Journal

ANN CLEAVES
Courtesy Palisadian Post (Calif.)

DALE STEPHANOS
Courtesy Boston Herald

## KIDS TODAY LACK PHYSICAL ACTIVITY

DAVE SATTLER
Courtesy Lafayette Journal Courier (Ind.)

169

ED GAMBLE
Courtesy Florida Times-Union

"You won't have to worry about my influence on your kids, anymore! I've decided to POLICE myself!"

RICHARD CROWSON
Courtesy Wichita Eagle

DON LANDGREN, JR.
Courtesy The Landmark (Mass.)

"...THERE'S SIX ZEROS IN A MILL— WAIT— WHAT DO YOU MEAN YOU'RE PLACING A BID TO BUY THE RED SOX?"

TOM GIBB
Courtesy The Tribune-Democrat

"AND, IN THE FUTURE, MANKIND WILL BE JOINED IN ONE INCREDIBLE, SEAMLESS FLASH-QUICK CYBER-CONNECTION. UNLESS SOME PUNK E-MAILER SHUTS IT DOWN!"

REX BABIN
Courtesy Sacramento Bee

THE SACRAMENTO BEE REXBABIN
HOLLYWOOD EXECS FOR
GORE

BOB GORRELL
Courtesy Creators Syndicate

GORRELL ©2000 CREATORS SYNDICATE INC WWW.TOONVILLE.COM
WITH TWO PERCENT OF THE VOTE COUNTED, WE PROJECT A RECOUNT OF ABSENTEE BALLOTS UNLESS A WINNER IS ERRONEOUSLY DECLARED BEFORE RETRACTING HIS CONCESSION...

MORE FUZZY MATH

Where AMERICA gets its Campaign NEWS
CRONKITE
'70s
RATHER
'80s
KING
'90s
LENO
'00s
JIMBORGMAN

JIM BORGMAN
Courtesy Cincinnati Enquirer

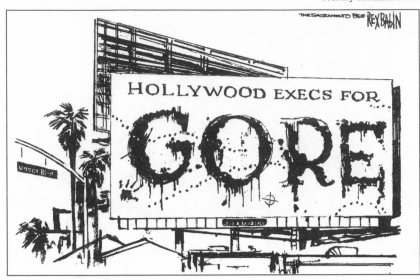

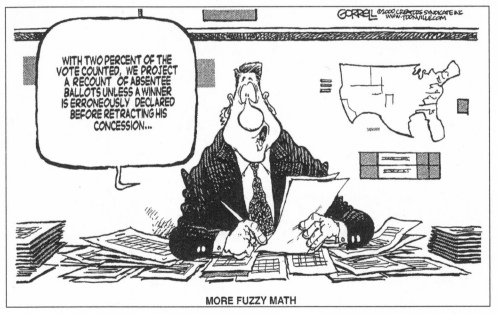

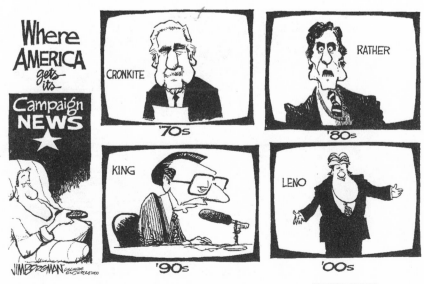

DAVID HORSEY
Courtesy Seattle Post-Intelligencer

· TEST AUDIENCE ·

STEVEN LAIT
Courtesy Oakland Tribune

S. C. RAWLS
Courtesy NEA

GEORGE DANBY
Courtesy Bangor Daily News

DAVID HARDIN COX
Courtesy Arkansas Democrat-Gazette

"ELIAN, HOW WOULD YOU FEEL ABOUT GOING BACK TO CUBA AND LEAVING THIS LAND OF FREEDOM?"

MARK THORNHILL
Courtesy North County Times (Calif.)

DALE STEPHANOS
Courtesy Boston Herald

176

# Canada

In spite of the government's toughened immigration policies, several boatloads of Chinese managed to enter the country, sparking renewed concern that Canada remains an easy target for illegal immigrants. Authorities also fear that terrorists consider Canada a safe haven. In fact, the government is aware of some 350 suspects linked to 50 radical groups. And the Royal Canadian Mounted Police continues to be unable to provide full protection for the prime minister, who was hit with a pie while on tour.

After eliminating the national deficit, Canada operated with a surplus that Minister Paul Martin found hard to pin a number on. It seemed to grow daily, but about $1 billion was said to have been mismanaged in human resources development.

As in the U.S., the cost of gasoline skyrocketed across the country. Aid that had been promised to farmers was not forthcoming. Many senior citizens from the U.S. began taking bus trips into Canada to purchase prescription drugs because they are much cheaper than at home.

Prime Minister Jean Chretien led his Liberal Party to a 106-seat victory in December parliamentary elections. Canada mourned the death of Pierre Elliot Trudeau, one of its most respected and beloved prime ministers.

Canadian focus groups disagree on icons for new currency design.

...just a suggestion.

ROY PETERSON
Courtesy Vancouver Sun

ROY PETERSON
Courtesy Vancouver Sun

TIM DOLIGHAN
Courtesy Toronto Sun

STEVE NEASE
Courtesy Niagara Falls Review

ANDY DONATO
Courtesy Toronto Sun

W. A. HOGAN
Courtesy Times-Transcript (New Bruns.)

ANDY DONATO
Courtesy Toronto Sun

FRED CURATOLO
Courtesy Edmonton Sun

W. A. HOGAN
Courtesy Times-Transcript (New Bruns.)

TIM DOLIGHAN
Courtesy Toronto Sun

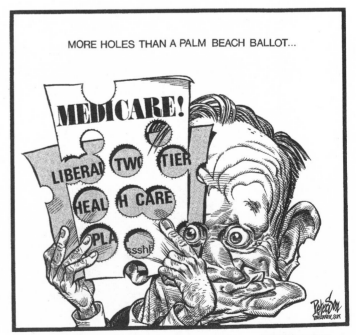

ROY PETERSON
Courtesy Vancouver Sun

STEVE NEASE
Courtesy Niagara Falls Review

STEVE NEASE
Courtesy Niagara Falls Review

STEVE WETZEL
Courtesy Harrisburg Patriot-News

HANK MCCLURE
Courtesy Lawton Constitution

RICK KOLLINGER
Courtesy Easton Star-Democrat (Md.)

# The Military

A $1 billion warship, the *USS Cole,* was attacked October 12 by terrorists while in the Yemen port of Aden. Two suicide bombers blew a 40-foot hole in the side of the ship, destroying a three-level engine room and killing 17 sailors and wounding many more.

Members of Congress immediately began an investigation to determine if the bombing might have been prevented, since the *Cole* was in the harbor simply for refueling. Some Republican lawmakers charged that the Clinton Administration's cutbacks in defense spending may have influenced the Navy's decision to use a high-risk port to refuel its vessels.

The Navy in October took part in NATO exercises on the Puerto Rican island of Vieques. The maneuvers by 50 ships and 31,000 soldiers from six countries were the largest in years. Ships fired missiles at the bombing range and staged an amphibious landing. Protesters stepped up their efforts to force the U.S. to withdraw its military presence on Vieques. President Clinton pledged that the Navy will leave Vieques by May 2003 if residents vote for expulsion.

BOB LANG
Courtesy The News-Sentinel (Ind.)

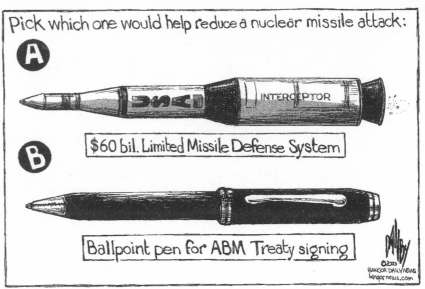

GEORGE DANBY
Courtesy Bangor Daily News

KIRK ANDERSON
Courtesy St. Paul Pioneer Press

NATIONAL MISSILE DEFENSE UMBRELLA

JOE HELLER
Courtesy Green Bay Press-Gazette

STEVE MCBRIDE
Courtesy Independence Daily Reporter (Kan.)

JAMES CASCIARI
Courtesy Vero Beach Press Journal

JAMES MCCLOSKEY
Courtesy Staunton Daily News Leader (Va.)

CHARLES M. (Sparky) SCHULZ
1922-2000

JOHN TREVER
Courtesy Albuquerque Journal

JEFF MacNelly, 1947-2000

# In Memoriam

A number of public figures passed away during the year, including actors Sir Alec Guinness, Walter Matthau, Sir John Gielgud, and Gwen Verdon, the multi-talented Steve Allen, and Dallas Cowboys football coach Tom Landry.

Also passing from the scene were two beloved giants of the cartooning world: Charles Schulz, creator of the nonpareil comic strip "Peanuts," and Jeff MacNelly, three-time winner of the Pulitzer Prize for editorial cartooning, creator of the comic strip "Shoe," and contributor to this annual for the past 28 years.

WILLIAM L. FLINT
Courtesy Arlington Morning News (Tex.)

JON RICHARDS
Courtesy Santa Fe Reporter

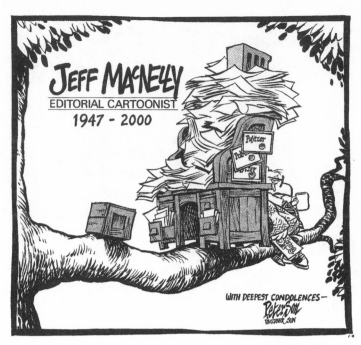

ROY PETERSON
Courtesy Vancouver Sun

DON MARQUIS
Courtesy Paradise Post (Calif.)

DAVID HORSEY
Courtesy Seattle Post-Intelligencer

DICK LOCHER
Courtesy Chicago Tribune

GARY VARVEL
Courtesy Indianapolis Star

DANIEL FENECH
Courtesy Saline Reporter (Mich.)

DOUG MACGREGOR
Courtesy News Press at Fort Myers

MARK STREETER
Courtesy Savannah Morning News

MARSHALL RAMSEY
Courtesy Jackson Clarion-Ledger (Miss.)

BRIAN DUFFY
Courtesy Des Moines Register

192

# . . . and Other Issues

The National Park Service set off a "controlled burn" in the Bandelier National Monument area which turned into an inferno that forced the evacuation of more than 20,000 people, destroyed 200 homes, and damaged hundreds of others. At one point, the fire came within 300 yards of a building at the Los Alamos National Laboratory where plutonium was stored.

Angry residents insisted that the National Park Service should not have started a controlled burn when New Mexico's fierce spring winds were blowing.

Some 670 million passengers boarded U.S. airlines during the year. That is more than double the 250 million passengers of just 20 years ago. Partly as a result of this rapid growth, complaints about flight delays, poor customer service, lost baggage, and overbooking increased exponentially.

Late in the year, the U.S. and Russia put the first crew in the International Space Station some 230 miles in the heavens, U.S. Navy SEAL William Shepherd and two Russians.

PETER DUNLAP-SHOHL
Courtesy Anchorage Daily News

"WASHINGTON WANTS TO KNOW, CAN WE SPEED THIS UP A LITTLE?"

WILLIAM L. FLINT
Courtesy Arlington Morning News (Tex.)

RICK MCKEE
Courtesy Augusta Chronicle

WAYNE STROOT
Courtesy Hastings Tribune

BILL WHITEHEAD
Courtesy Kansas City Business Journal

MICKEY SIPORIN
Courtesy Los Angeles Times

ANN CLEAVES
Courtesy Palisadian Post (Calif.)

JOEL PETT
Courtesy Lexington Herald-Leader

SANDY CAMPBELL
Courtesy The Tennessean

TIM HARTMAN
Courtesy The Valley News (Pa.)

ETTA HULME
Courtesy Fort Worth Star-Telegram

ETTA @ 2000 FORT WORTH STAR-TELEGRAM
HULME

"FIRST ONE TO DIE BEFORE THE DEATH TAX IS REPEALED IS A ROTTEN EGG"

JIMMY MARGULIES
Courtesy Hackensack Record

WAYNE STROOT
Courtesy Black Hills Pioneer (S.D.)

ETTA HULME
Courtesy Fort Worth Star-Telegram

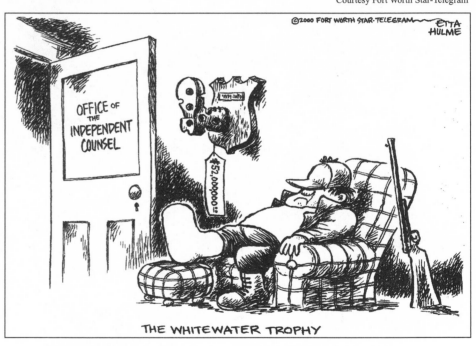

MIKE KEEFE
Courtesy Denver Post

BILL GARNER
Courtesy Washington Times

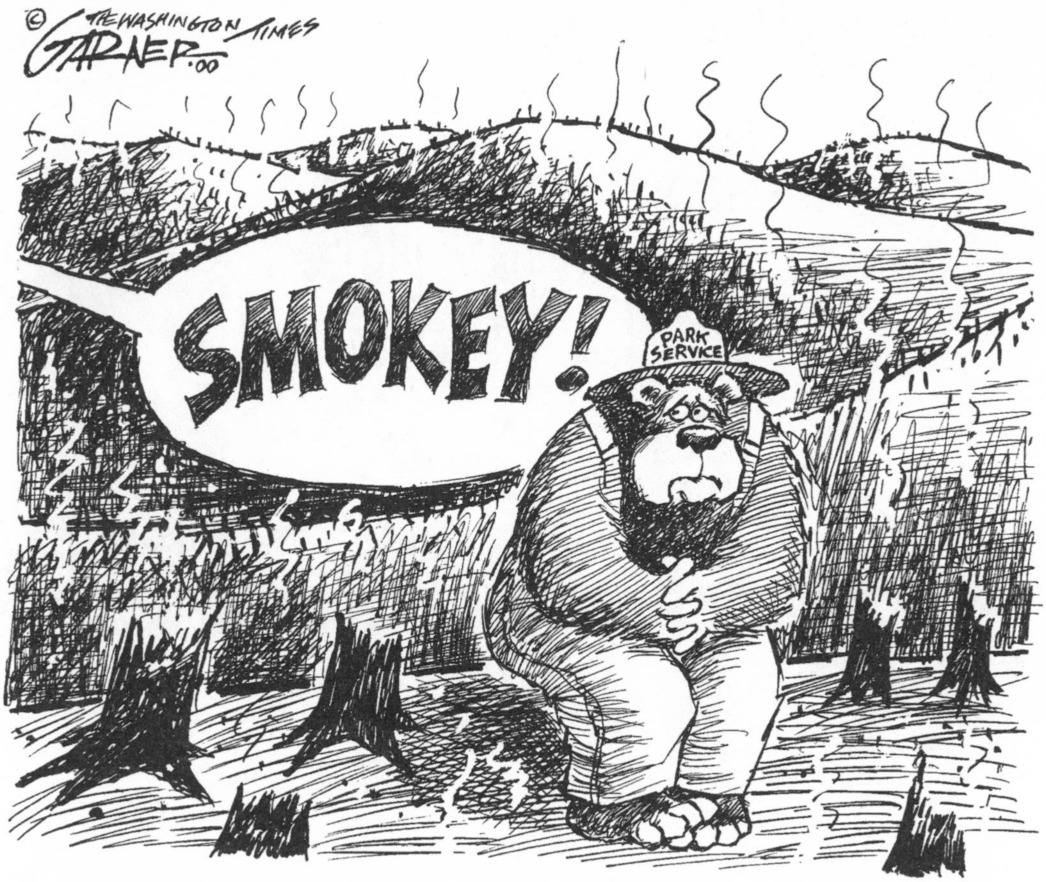
© THE WASHINGTON TIMES GARNER '00
SMOKEY!
PARK SERVICE

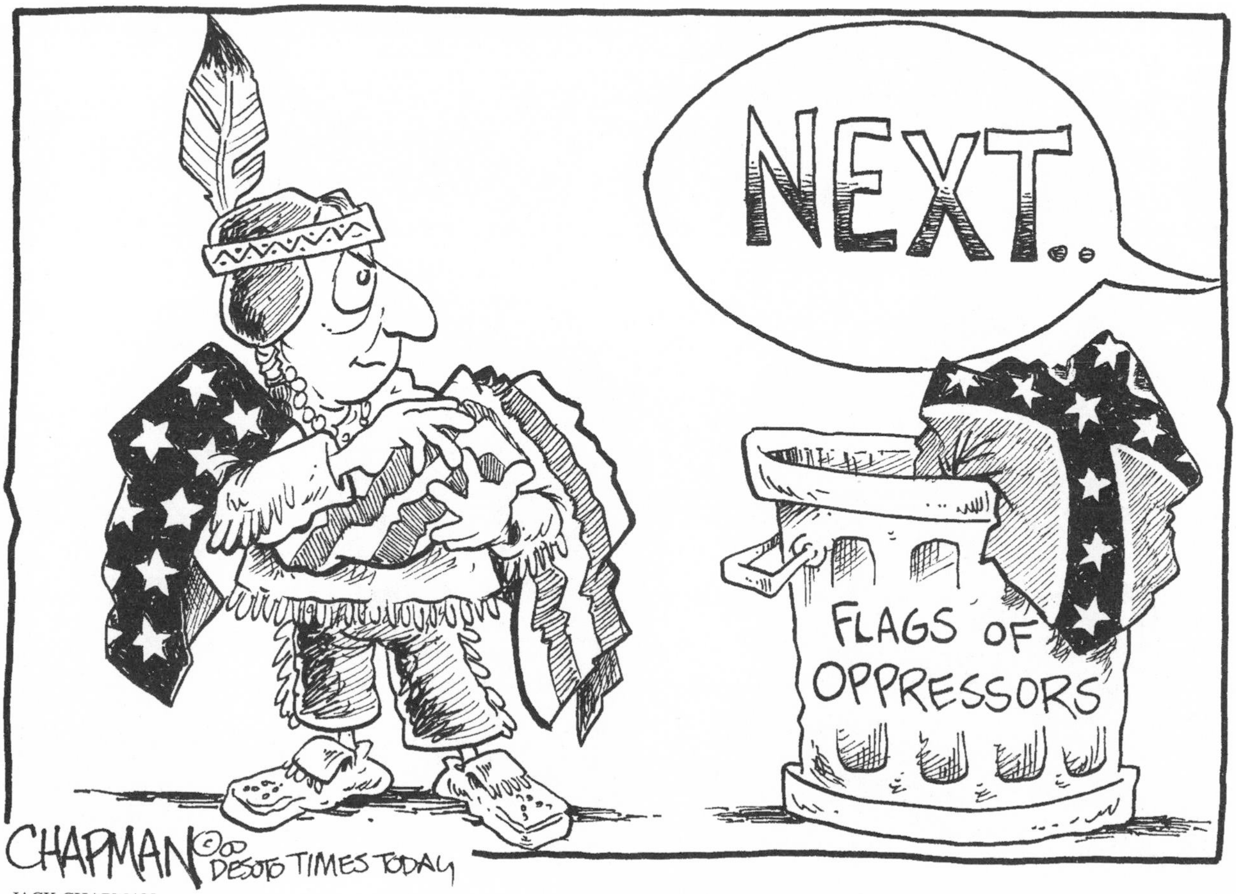
NEXT..
FLAGS OF OPPRESSORS
CHAPMAN ©'00 DESOTO TIMES TODAY

JACK CHAPMAN
Courtesy Desoto Times Today (Miss.)

MIKE KEEFE
Courtesy Denver Post

RICKY NOBILE
Courtesy Bolivar Commercial (Miss.)

# Past Award Winners

## PULITZER PRIZE

1922—Rollin Kirby, New York World
1923—No award given
1924—J.N. Darling, New York Herald-Tribune
1925—Rollin Kirby, New York World
1926—D.R. Fitzpatrick, St. Louis Post-Dispatch
1927—Nelson Harding, Brooklyn Eagle
1928—Nelson Harding, Brooklyn Eagle
1929—Rollin Kirby, New York World
1930—Charles Macauley, Brooklyn Eagle
1931—Edmund Duffy, Baltimore Sun
1932—John T. McCutcheon, Chicago Tribune
1933—H.M. Talburt, Washington Daily News
1934—Edmund Duffy, Baltimore Sun
1935—Ross A. Lewis, Milwaukee Journal
1936—No award given
1937—C.D. Batchelor, New York Daily News
1938—Vaughn Shoemaker, Chicago Daily News
1939—Charles G. Werner, Daily Oklahoman
1940—Edmund Duffy, Baltimore Sun
1941—Jacob Burck, Chicago Times
1942—Herbert L. Block, NEA
1943—Jay N. Darling, New York Herald-Tribune
1944—Clifford K. Berryman, Washington Star
1945—Bill Mauldin, United Features Syndicate
1946—Bruce Russell, Los Angeles Times
1947—Vaughn Shoemaker, Chicago Daily News
1948—Reuben L. ("Rube") Goldberg, New York Sun
1949—Lute Pease, Newark Evening News
1950—James T. Berryman, Washington Star
1951—Reginald W. Manning, Arizona Republic
1952—Fred L. Packer, New York Mirror
1953—Edward D. Kuekes, Cleveland Plain Dealer
1954—Herbert L. Block, Washington Post
1955—Daniel R. Fitzpatrick, St. Louis Post-Dispatch
1956—Robert York, Louisville Times
1957—Tom Little, Nashville Tennessean
1958—Bruce M. Shanks, Buffalo Evening News
1959—Bill Mauldin, St. Louis Post-Dispatch
1960—No award given
1961—Carey Orr, Chicago Tribune
1962—Edmund S. Valtman, Hartford Times
1963—Frank Miller, Des Moines Register
1964—Paul Conrad, Denver Post
1965—No award given
1966—Don Wright, Miami News
1967—Patrick B. Oliphant, Denver Post
1968—Eugene Gray Payne, Charlotte Observer
1969—John Fischetti, Chicago Daily News
1970—Thomas F. Darcy, Newsday
1971—Paul Conrad, Los Angeles Times
1972—Jeffrey K. MacNelly, Richmond News Leader
1973—No award given
1974—Paul Szep, Boston Globe
1975—Garry Trudeau, Universal Press Syndicate
1976—Tony Auth, Philadelphia Enquirer
1977—Paul Szep, Boston Globe

1978—Jeff MacNelly, Richmond News Leader
1979—Herbert Block, Washington Post
1980—Don Wright, Miami News
1981—Mike Peters, Dayton Daily News
1982—Ben Sargent, Austin American-Statesman
1983—Dick Locher, Chicago Tribune
1984—Paul Conrad, Los Angeles Times
1985—Jeff MacNelly, Chicago Tribune
1986—Jules Feiffer, Universal Press Syndicate
1987—Berke Breathed, Washington Post Writers Group
1988—Doug Marlette, Atlanta Constitution
1989—Jack Higgins, Chicago Sun-Times
1990—Tom Toles, Buffalo News
1991—Jim Borgman, Cincinnati Enquirer
1992—Signe Wilkinson, Philadelphia Daily News
1993—Steve Benson, Arizona Republic
1994—Michael Ramirez, Memphis Commercial Appeal
1995—Mike Luckovich, Atlanta Constitution
1996—Jim Morin, Miami Herald
1997—Walt Handelsman, New Orleans Times-Picayune
1998—Steve Breen, Asbury Park Press
1999—David Horsey, Seattle Post-Intelligencer
2000—Joel Pett, Lexington Herald-Leader

## NATIONAL SOCIETY OF PROFESSIONAL JOURNALISTS AWARD (SIGMA DELTA CHI AWARD)

1942—Jacob Burck, Chicago Times
1943—Charles Werner, Chicago Sun
1944—Henry Barrow, Associated Press
1945—Reuben L. Goldberg, New York Sun
1946—Dorman H. Smith, NEA
1947—Bruce Russell, Los Angeles Times
1948—Herbert Block, Washington Post
1949—Herbert Block, Washington Post
1950—Bruce Russell, Los Angeles Times
1951—Herbert Block, Washington Post and
     Bruce Russell, Los Angeles Times
1952—Cecil Jensen, Chicago Daily News
1953—John Fischetti, NEA
1954—Calvin Alley, Memphis Commercial Appeal
1955—John Fischetti, NEA
1956—Herbert Block, Washington Post
1957—Scott Long, Minneapolis Tribune
1958—Clifford H. Baldowski, Atlanta Constitution
1959—Charles G. Brooks, Birmingham News
1960—Dan Dowling, New York Herald-Tribune
1961—Frank Interlandi, Des Moines Register
1962—Paul Conrad, Denver Post
1963—William Mauldin, Chicago Sun-Times
1964—Charles Bissell, Nashville Tennessean
1965—Roy Justus, Minneapolis Star
1966—Patrick Oliphant, Denver Post

1967—Eugene Payne, Charlotte Observer
1968—Paul Conrad, Los Angeles Times
1969—William Mauldin, Chicago Sun-Times
1970—Paul Conrad, Los Angeles Times
1971—Hugh Haynie, Louisville Courier-Journal
1972—William Mauldin, Chicago Sun-Times
1973—Paul Szep, Boston Globe
1974—Mike Peters, Dayton Daily News
1975—Tony Auth, Philadelphia Enquirer
1976—Paul Szep, Boston Globe
1977—Don Wright, Miami News
1978—Jim Borgman, Cincinnati Enquirer
1979—John P. Trever, Albuquerque Journal
1980—Paul Conrad, Los Angeles Times
1981—Paul Conrad, Los Angeles Times
1982—Dick Locher, Chicago Tribune
1983—Rob Lawlor, Philadelphia Daily News
1984—Mike Lane, Baltimore Evening Sun
1985—Doug Marlette, Charlotte Observer
1986—Mike Keefe, Denver Post
1987—Paul Conrad, Los Angeles Times
1988—Jack Higgins, Chicago Sun-Times
1989—Don Wright, Palm Beach Post
1990—Jeff MacNelly, Chicago Tribune
1991—Walt Handelsman, New Orleans Times-Picayune
1992—Robert Ariail, Columbia State
1993—Herbert Block, Washington Post
1994—Jim Borgman, Cincinnati Enquirer
1995—Michael Ramirez, Memphis Commercial Appeal
1996—Paul Conrad, Los Angeles Times
1997—Michael Ramirez, Los Angeles Times
1998—Jack Higgins, Chicago Sun-Times
1999—Mike Thompson, Detroit Free Press

## FISCHETTI AWARD

1982—Lee Judge, Kansas City Times
1983—Bill DeOre, Dallas Morning News
1984—Tom Toles, Buffalo News
1985—Scott Willis, Dallas Times-Herald
1986—Doug Marlette, Charlotte Observer
1987—Dick Locher, Chicago Tribune
1988—Arthur Bok, Akron Beacon-Journal
1989—Lambert Der, Greenville News
1990—Jeff Stahler, Cincinnati Post
1991—Mike Keefe, Denver Post
1992—Doug Marlette, New York Newsday
1993—Bill Schorr, Kansas City Star
1994—John Deering, Arkansas Democrat-Gazette
1995—Stuart Carlson, Milwaukee Journal Sentinel
1996—Jimmy Margulies, The Record, New Jersey
1997—Gary Markstein, Milwaukee Journal Sentinel
1998—Jack Higgins, Chicago Sun-Times
1999—Nick Anderson, Louisville Courier-Journal
2000—Jim Morin, Miami Herald

## NATIONAL NEWSPAPER AWARD/CANADA

1949—Jack Boothe, Toronto Globe and Mail
1950—James G. Reidford, Montreal Star
1951—Len Norris, Vancouver Sun
1952—Robert La Palme, Le Devoir, Montreal
1953—Robert W. Chambers, Halifax Chronicle-Herald
1954—John Collins, Montreal Gazette
1955—Merle R. Tingley, London Free Press
1956—James G. Reidford, Toronto Globe and Mail
1957—James G. Reidford, Toronto Globe and Mail
1958—Raoul Hunter, Le Soleil, Quebec
1959—Duncan Macpherson, Toronto Star
1960—Duncan Macpherson, Toronto Star
1961—Ed McNally, Montreal Star
1962—Duncan Macpherson, Toronto Star
1963—Jan Kamienski, Winnipeg Tribune
1964—Ed McNally, Montreal Star
1965—Duncan Macpherson, Toronto Star
1966—Robert W. Chambers, Halifax Chronicle-Herald
1967—Raoul Hunter, Le Soleil, Quebec
1968—Roy Peterson, Vancouver Sun
1969—Edward Uluschak, Edmonton Journal
1970—Duncan Macpherson, Toronto Daily Star
1971—Yardley Jones, Toronto Daily Star
1972—Duncan Macpherson, Toronto Star
1973—John Collins, Montreal Gazette
1974—Blaine, Hamilton Spectator
1975—Roy Peterson, Vancouver Sun
1976—Andy Donato, Toronto Sun
1977—Terry Mosher, Montreal Gazette
1978—Terry Mosher, Montreal Gazette
1979—Edd Uluschak, Edmonton Journal
1980—Vic Roschkov, Toronto Star
1981—Tom Innes, Calgary Herald
1982—Blaine, Hamilton Spectator
1983—Dale Cummings, Winnipeg Free Press
1984—Roy Peterson, Vancouver Sun
1985—Ed Franklin, Toronto Globe and Mail
1986—Brian Gable, Regina Leader-Post
1987—Raffi Anderian, Ottawa Citizen
1988—Vance Rodewalt, Calgary Herald
1989—Cameron Cardow, Regina Leader-Post
1990—Roy Peterson, Vancouver Sun
1991—Guy Badeaux, Le Droit, Ottawa
1992—Bruce Mackinnon, Halifax Herald
1993—Bruce Mackinnon, Halifax Herald
1994—Roy Peterson, Vancouver Sun
1995—Brian Gable, Toronto Globe and Mail
1996—Roy Peterson, Vancouver Sun
1997—Serge Chapleau, La Presse
1998—Roy Peterson, Vancouver Sun
1999—Serge Chapleau, La Presse

# Index of Cartoonists

# INDEX OF CARTOONISTS